D0881354

The Universal Drum

The participation in a dance . . . exhibits a wonderful unison; [the dancers] are, as it were, fused into a single being stirred by a single impulse . . . the universal drum. . . .

—Louis Robinson

All living creatures are constantly consummating their own rhythm.

—Jean D'Udine

The Universal Drum

Dance Imagery
in the Poetry of
Eliot, Crane, Roethke, and Williams

Audrey T. Rodgers

The Pennsylvania State University Press
University Park and London

Portions of Chapters 2, 3, and 5 have appeared
in *Criticism*, *Arizona Quarterly*, and *Four Decades*.

Library of Congress Cataloging in Publication Data

Rodgers, Audrey T
    The universal drum.
    Bibliography: p. 191.
    Includes index.
    1. American poetry—20th century—History and criticism.
    2. Dancing in literature. I. Title.
PS324.R64 811'.5'40915   79-12480
ISBN 0-271-00220-4

for Ann & Bart

Contents

Acknowledgments

I welcome this chance to thank both friends and colleagues who have read parts of this book and who have offered me their invaluable insights, encouragement, and good wishes. They include Professors Henry Sams, Stanley Weintraub, and Robert Secor of The Pennsylvania State University. I am grateful as well for the careful reading of the manuscript by Professor Eric Domville of the University of Toronto and for his important suggestions and observations. I owe a special thanks to Mr. John Pickering of the University Press, whose patient and astute reading of the book was greatly appreciated.

I should like to thank the Institute for Arts and Humanistic Studies and the Liberal Arts College Fund for Research at Penn State under the guidance of Dean Thomas Magner for several grants that furthered the research phase of this study.

On a more personal level, I am profoundly indebted to my parents, David and Beck Tropauer, who introduced me to poetry before I could read. Most importantly, I thank my husband, Allan Rodgers, whose quiet confidence in me has been the loving bulwark of my professional life, and whose patience during the writing of this book was boundless.

Finally, I am grateful to the poets whose work I have studied here: Eliot, Crane, Roethke, and Williams for giving me an experience of mystery and delight.

It is difficult
to get the news from poems
yet men die miserably every day
for lack
of what is found there.
Wm. Carlos Williams

Introduction

The story of dance imagery in the poetry of Eliot, Crane, Roethke, and Williams is the subject of this book. Even a cursory examination of their verse reveals immediately that the dance figures largely as both image and symbol. It is difficult to find a poet in the twentieth century who did not, in e. e. cummings's terms, sing his didn't and dance his did; indeed, the poetry of Auden, Berryman, Snyder, Lowell, Schwartz, and Levertov is suffused with dance images. One might even argue that the dance was, after all, man's first way of communicating as well as his first art. But the four poets whose work I explore here are chosen primarily because the image of the dance is *central* to their perception of experience.

The dance was important to them as *one* means for expressing a complex set of emotional and intellectual states. Each was caught up with the efficacy of kinetic activity; each explored ways to delineate the ineffable experience in the image of the dance; each was deeply affected by myth and ritual; and each was in search of a "transcendent" experience he perceived the *art* of the dance to have achieved. This *poetic* ideal was related neither to Emerson's transcendental vision nor to any other specific doctrinal conviction but to the quest for a harmonizing experience that transformed the fragments of the modern world, where, as they individually testified, man had lost his way. For Eliot "transcendence" frequently meant the awareness of the potentiality for "serenity, stillness, and reconciliation"; for Crane the sense of a Platonic wholeness; for Roethke the recognition of the impalpable mystery underlying all living things, himself included; and

1

for Williams the union of the imagination with the "things" of quotidian reality. In Whitmanesque spirit, each sought to be the "arbiter of the diverse." As craftsmen, each of these poets understood the integrative function of Yeats's dancer and saw in the image a means for revealing universal accord. "And everything comes to One,/As we dance on, dance on, dance on," Roethke celebrates.

All of the poets I examine in this book were sensitive to developments in both ballet and modern dance; each knew a distinguished dancer and revered such artists as Duncan, Nijinsky, Portapovitch, and Graham. An interesting facet of my investigations led to the discovery that modern dance and early twentieth-century American poetry developed in the same artistic climate and celebrated those decades with a freshness, vivacity, and originality not experienced since Whitman. I have felt it important to indicate the innovations in the dance as they parallel congenial innovations in modern poetry. The poets I have chosen, despite their European links to such movements as *Symbolisme* and despite Eliot's changed loyalties, were essentially American poets whose roots were in the same native ground that gave birth to American dance—in the pioneering work of Isadora and others. However, it would be a questionable premise to assume that modern dance "created" modern poetry! It is more reasonable to say that both arts shared a compatible vision. Both dancer and poet, as I shall demonstrate, shared an impulse to impose order—a *new* order, as Pound declared—upon the universal chaos they perceived around them. However, it should be noted that all artists, in all ages, set for themselves this lofty goal. More significantly, the goal led dancers and poets alike, in this period, *away* from the nineteenth century's notions of order to create their own. The dance, as an image of poetry, offered one perspective by which the imagination reshaped "reality."

This book is, by design, limited in scope. I hasten to stress that no premise exists to suggest that poetry *is* imagery.

Indeed, what a poem *is* has been the subject of a persistent dialectic for at least two centuries, and there is little inclination to shut off the lively debate. Poetry has been called a dynamic of sensuous forms, or emotive language, or an object whose unity is revealed, as Coleridge said, "in the balance and reconciliation of opposites or discordant elements: of sameness with difference; of the general, with the concrete; the idea, with the image." Williams called the poem "a small (or large) machine made of words"; Crane saw the poem as an expression of "concepts in the more direct terms of physical-psychic experience." However poets muse on the delicate and elusive definitions of poetry, there seems to be little disagreement about the elements that comprise it: composition, language, rhythm, and a tension that gives to poetry its dramatic quality. The poets I deal with here knew of Valéry's concern with refining "poetic diction"; they developed new approaches to metaphor and symbol; they discussed the "scaffolding" of such epics as the *Commedia* and *Ulysses*—anxious to use them as models; they looked upon traditional prosody with challenge and focused on the dynamic aspects of language, whether lyrical or discordant as suited their purposes. They redefined the image with a precision and complexity not known before in American poetry.

Yet, what always "mattered" as Eliot pointed out was the "whole poem." These poets discussed *poetry* enthusiastically but assiduously avoided analyzing their own individual work. Williams could say of Marianne Moore, "Miss Moore gets great pleasure from wiping soiled words or cutting them clean out, removing the aureoles that have been pasted about them or taking them bodily from greasy contexts," but he fell into stony silence when any "symbolism" in *Paterson* was broached.

Without offering an exhaustive analysis of the crucial ingredients of poetry—structure, metrics, diction—I have, nevertheless, touched upon them when such elements are linked indissolubly to dance imagery. A necessary distortion, it is hoped, yields its own riches.

Still another limitation need be recognized. This study is neither a literary history nor a philosophy of the dance. No attempt has been made to trace modern dance, only insofar as dance pioneers such as Isadora, Diaghilev, and others stirred the imagination of the age. I have indicated where the two developing arts, modern dance and modern poetry, touched common chords, and I have indicated, as well, how the traditions of such giants as Whitman and Yeats served as reinforcement through *their* choice of the dance as a significant image for poetry. Much of the early part of this book is an effort to recreate the exciting sense, for the poet, that the dance was everywhere. It is no accident that Eliot, Crane, Roethke, and Williams chose the dance as an image to shore against their ruins; as late as 1955, Williams would affirm, "Poetry began with the measure, it began with the dance."

CHAPTER I

The Poet as Dancer

This book began with the discovery that the dance is a recurrent image in the poetry of four American poets: T. S. Eliot, Hart Crane, Theodore Roethke, and William Carlos Williams. "I hear my being dance from ear to ear," Theodore Roethke wrote. For each of these poets, the dance was to become a significant motif in the expression of his innermost thoughts and feelings. At times, the dance was a reflection of cosmic harmony and interior balance; at other times, it was the frenzied activity of a maddened and disordered world. In still other moments, it was a form of prayer and humility, not far in spirit from the dancing dervish in Crete who tells the young Kazantzakis: "If a man cannot dance, he cannot pray. Angels have mouths but lack the power of speech. They speak to God by dancing." Moreover, "dancing kills the ego, and once the ego has been killed there is no further obstacle to prevent you from joining with God."[1]

The definition of the dance as *rhythmic patterns of movement* acquired in the poetry of Eliot, Crane, Roethke, and Williams a wide spectrum of associations that find their parallel in primitive ritual, in formal ballet, and in the fresh new interpretations by the dancers in the late nineteenth and early twentieth centuries. Ezra Pound's poetic summons to "make it new!" encouraged poets to experiment with dance images that resulted in rich symbolic overtones and novel perspectives. They took Yeats's dancer many moods deeper; they extended Whitman's fine frenzy many circles wider. Always intent on expressing the often inexpressible, these poets achieved with dance images a vehicle for penetrating "the way feelings, emotions, and all other subjective experiences come and go—their rise and growth, their intricate synthesis that gives our inner life unity and personality."[2]

The poets I am considering were troubled by their ambivalence toward the past, their alienation in the present, and their despair for the future. From its inception, their poetry sought to harmonize the fragments of the contemporary world; the rebellion against stale traditions combined with an equal insistence on "continuity." Their poetry is distinguished by a search—in spite of all the facts of contemporary life—for those ineffable moments of faith, wholeness, and balance poets termed "reality." "Everything we do is an effort to achieve conjunction,"[3] Williams told philosopher Stanley Moore. They sought new metaphors to express that "conjunction"; perhaps it was to be imaged "in the still point of the turning world" or in "one Bridge of Fire" or in the mind that "dances with itself,/taking you by the hand." If the twentieth century seemed "waiting for its poet," as Emerson had proclaimed, the new poetry would of necessity embark on a search for new *modes* to define its experience. The poet, Williams declared, must "break up the fixities of words and make them flow together like figures in a dance."

The invention of dance images in the poetry of Eliot, Crane, Roethke, and Williams seems an outcome of a scrupulous concern with words, a response to an awakening modern consciousness of myths and rituals, and the need to reach *beyond* the logic of the intellect. Moreover, that dance could convey an intricate network of experiences was demonstrated by Isadora Duncan and Mary Wigman, Martha Graham and Michel Fokine, and a host of dancers and choreographers who followed them. Even Charlie Chaplin, transcending the limitations of language, provided a model—his pantomime is most often called a "dance." So it was that the achievements of dance and ballet at the turn of the century and after were

6

cheering incentives to poets searching for a confirmation of their own creative efforts.

The poets whose work I examine disagreed more often than they agreed on matters of faith; their viewpoints on the function of the imagination seem frequently incompatible. Often their artistic techniques seem widely diverse. Yet all these individual perspectives do not obscure their quintessential preoccupation: to discover an order beneath the surface of visible things. The story of the dance in their poetry is the subject of this study. What we find is not only a profusion of dance images, but widely divergent associations that dance held for each of them. Each seems aware that "before words were, and when words failed him, man danced,"[4] creating order anew.

Poet and Dancer

A remarkable event occurred in the autumn of 1922 when Isadora Duncan danced before a stunned audience in Cleveland, Ohio. Her program was based on Tchaikovsky, and at the close of the *Pathétique*, as she stood naked-breasted and radiantly defiant before the crowd of nine thousand, the silence was broken only by the wild clapping of one lone admirer. So Hart Crane,[5] then twenty-three, recalls his first response to Isadora, her "plastic grace" lost on most of those morally outraged theater-goers. She took the occasion to remind them to read Walt Whitman's "Calamus," summoning up Whitman's own efforts more than sixty years before to move "in paths untrodden."

For Isadora, the experience—repeated in other American cities—was a bitter confirmation that her own country had still not come of age. The American reception, which alternated between icy silence and loud catcalls, was an ironic contrast to her European triumphs in the first decades of the century when she was the darling of Paris—the modern

Athena of the Gaieté-Lyrique. At forty-four, only five years before her sudden death, the audiences at home marching out in indignant protest signaled a rejection precisely where she had craved acceptance.

For Hart Crane, exuberant at the spectacle of Isadora, whom he described as a "flaming gale . . . a wave of life," the event was a romantic affirmation of the alienated artist who could, as he had declared in "Chaplinesque," "evade you, and all else but the heart." Years later, he would celebrate Isadora in *The Bridge*, including in his vision another artist who had known isolation and despair:

> In one last angelus lift throbbing throat—
> Listen, transmuting silence with that stilly note
> Of pain that Emily, that Isadora knew!

It is Isadora's words that introduce the apocalyptic view of a fallen America to "Quaker Hill": "I see only the ideal. But no ideals have ever been fully successful on this earth."

To those who cherish "artifacts," the Cleveland event furnishes a savory bit of memorabilia for the scrapbook of literary history. More importantly, the image of Whitman, Isadora, and Crane symbolizes the shared destiny of poetry and the dance in the twentieth century. Here conjoined were the spiritual father of modern verse who, in Pound's tribute, "broke the new wood"; the "first apostle of freedom and democracy"[6] in the dance; and the exhilarated poet, still in 1922 "a man of no fortune, and with a name to come." The icon is fitting for an age disposed to rebels. Modern poetry and modern dance grew from the same soil and were stirred by the same impulses.

The wealth of dance images in American poetry testifies to the deepening bond between poet and dancer as each searched new ways to express the American experience. In their desire to liberate themselves from the dead hand of the past, to speak an American idiom, to create images of beauty and honesty, and—above all—in their zeal to bring their art to the people, Whitman and Isadora, with all their flamboyant genius, had believed quite literally in the American Dream. They interchanged images: the poet danced and the dancer created poems. Whitman prophesied the kinship when he sang, "I am a dance. . . . Play up there! the fit is whirling me fast!" Isadora wrote: "I bring you the dance . . . where have I discovered it? By the Pacific Ocean, by the waving pine forests of the Sierra Nevada. I have seen the ideal figure of youthful America dancing over the top of the Rockies. . . . I am indeed the spiritual daughter of Walt Whitman."[7]* Years after he saw Isadora in Cleveland, Crane as the poet dances with Pocahontas in *The Bridge*, reminding the Indian Maquokeeta: "We danced, O Brave . . . we danced." Tracing the trajectory cast by Whitman and Isadora, we discover dance images that convey a multiplicity of meanings as the poet tested new modes to communicate his perplexed states and to penetrate an often hostile and terrifying world. He was to discover in the dance a dynamic image, one—to borrow from Pound's "vorticism"—"from which, and through which, and into which, ideas are constantly rushing."

The goals declared by those who pioneered modern dance bear a striking resemblance to the ideas espoused by Pound, Eliot, and others at the forefront of the new poetry before World War I. Poets and dancers called for sweeping change. Both were self-conscious in that they were aware of their "developing arts"; and while at times theory was a means for explicating achieved novel effects, quite often practice served to illustrate fresh ideas.

*Isadora's first appearance in New York in 1899 was an interpretation of *The Rubaiyat* of Omar Khayyam, her expression of "poetry into dance." By "pose and dance" Isadora, like a "Greek statue," was a happy fusion of poetry and gesture. Her lifelong appreciation of the relationship between poetry, sculpture, and dance often produced such dances. See Macdougall, *Isadora*, 1960, pp. 36 ff.

The hallmark of both movements was an irrepressible freedom, whether in overthrowing usages of the immediate past or in seeking to *include* the data of the real world. Both were marked by innovation as each decade of poets and dancers experimented with theme and form. Dance historians note the inception of modernism in both ballet and dance with the scrapping of the tutu and the ballet slippers and the devotion to a greater concern with "the abstraction of things felt than with pictorial representation of things seen."[8] Similarly, the poets whose work I am considering here declared their liberation from Victorian constraints, from the rigidity of traditional poetic diction of the nineteenth century and the "old rules" of prosody.* *Pattern* would be transformed. A new concept of form stressed the line, and the "inner" structure, and the precision of the image. The new poetry tended to juxtapose surface fragmentation with inner form. Eliot firmly supported Pound's assertion that "any work of art is a compound of freedom and order," that "art hangs between chaos on the one side and mechanics on the other."[9]

In this way both modern dance and modern poetry sought to image the discontinuity, the rough texture of life, that seemed an intrinsic quality of the American experience, while validating the search for unity and design in art. The fragments and irregular verse, the "broken rhythms, off-balances, imperfect cadences,"[10] were alternated with formal, regular patterns and precise studied gestures. They sought a form, in short, that approximated the truths both of their innermost states and the *reality* they perceived around them.

The posing of opposites reinforced the tension of ideas and ranges of feelings both arts dramatized: polarities at once intellectual and emotional, spiritual and worldly, romantic and realistic. In dance, realism expressed itself in

---

*Williams would later regret the initial disowning of measure and devise for his poetry a more "satisfactory" form. He wrote in 1924 in "The Florida": "And we thought to escape rime / by imitation of the senseless / unarrangement of wild things—"

new attitudes toward space: the tendency *not* to defy gravity through dazzling acrobatic gestures, but to move with it and conquer it. Dance analysts often distinguish modern dance from classical ballet in the attitude toward the "floor": ballet pushing off the floor in an effort to transcend the limitations of space, and modern dance *using* the floor, returning to it as a necessary source of energy, a metaphor often for the earth itself.* In poetry, realism was best expressed by the inclusion of the tangible objects of the world: "No ideas but in things," Williams preached, and again in Frost: "The fact is the sweetest dream that labor knows." Realism also implied a Dionysian approach to the world embodied by the city (as Monroe Spears[12] demonstrated), by the tragedy of two wars, and by the poet's becoming "the spokesman for the existential moment."[13]

"Romanticism" stemmed from a preoccupation with the image, an argument Frank Kermode has made with much eloquence,[14] although the term "romantic" applied to modern poetry is often misleading. Seeking to externalize complex states in concise, epigrammatic, and sometimes harsh and violent images, modern poetry and modern dance cannot be viewed as traditionally romantic. Yet both movements reached back in human memory to an idyllic time when man seemed in closer harmony with natural things—in primitive myths and rites—and a "visionary" aura seems to have imbued the artist of both poetry and dance. The "imagism" that characterized both arts appears to have been an attempt to grapple with the imprecision of ideas in dance and poetry and lead them back to an experience of deeper "truth" and exact statement. Jean Erdman equated dance with the nonverbal poetic image. She wrote, "An idea for a dance can be sometimes stated in words. Many dancers, indeed, work from a script. But the idea, this thing that can be talked

*In Greek myth, King Antaeus of Libya, son of Poseidon and Mother Earth, was an accomplished athlete whose strength was renewed each time he touched the earth.[11]

about, must be realized in immediate physical terms. The dance itself, then, becomes a direct image of something that was formerly invisible."[15]

A need to mirror the inner self—another kind of "reality"—led to the inclination to transmute the experience of the ordinary world into poetry as well as into dance. In this sense, romanticism has a more fitting application. Perhaps the most important shared quality of these distinctive arts was a conscious return to myth and ritual. They seemed to acknowledge the truth of Nietzsche's observation that "every culture that has lost myth has lost, by the same token, its natural, healthy creativity; only a horizon ringed around with myth can unify a culture."[16]

It is probable that modern dance and modern poetry would have developed differently had it not been for the remarkable contemporary interest in myth and rite. What has been called a mythic renaissance was manifested in the search into myth by both scientist and humanist alike. Developments in anthropology, comparative mythology, psychology, and philosophy, with their rediscovery of primitive societies, their disclosure of archetypes and primordial myths, their revelations of contemporary human behavior in terms of these patterns—all served to stimulate the creative imagination of the artist. Artists discovered not only Frazer and Malinowski but Vico and Lévy-Bruhl. They followed avidly the debate over myth theory and were moved as much by Schliemann's discovery of the artifacts of Troy as by notions popularized by current interest in Freud and Jung. Moreover, they were drawn into a search for the American Myth hinted at earlier by Washington Irving, Fenimore Cooper, Hawthorne, and Melville. In myth they would find new forms, images, and themes. No less significant than the new way to order artistic form was the quest for belief in a hostile and unresponsive world, and both poet and dancer found a new "ideal" in myth's transcendent objective. "Unto to us lowliest sometimes sweep, descend/And of the curveship lend

12

a myth to God," Hart Crane's invocation concludes as he launched what he called the American Myth: *The Bridge.*

Repudiating what they deemed parochial views of their immediate predecessors, world-conscious in their outlook, poet and dancer expanded their horizons to include myths and rituals of primitive peoples, as well as those of highly developed cultures in the East. They searched both the recondite and the familiar, seeking new modes for presenting the vastly complex, discordant elements in the modern world, where as Williams testified there was "no one/to witness/and adjust, no one to drive the car." Whether through Whitman's or Crane's visionary company or Ruth St. Denis's Indian dances, "modernism" in both arts looked paradoxically backward to beginnings when in the timeless moment of creation man had been whole. Archetypal myths, validating that eternal moment, were dramatized in rituals, for, as the primitive knows, "nature yields nothing without ceremonies."[17] All man's rituals are a means toward the achievement of the world posited by myth; dance rites frequently celebrate man's transcendence of the barrier between himself and God and restore his identification with the original source of life.

No writer on myth has explained the significance of ritual more effectively than Mircea Eliade. Eliade has provided contemporary critics with important insights into the nature of primitive ritual as well as a collage of images that have stimulated the poetic imagination in the past. To know the origins of things—by reenactment through rituals—is to reenter primordial time and participate in the timelessness of cosmogony. Eliade places particular emphasis upon the rite of renewal implicit in the Myth of the Eternal Return: to create the world anew in endless cycles of death and rebirth is to achieve a form of immortality.

Similarly, Susanne Langer has stressed the importance of ritual as the "symbolic transformation of experiences that no other medium can adequately express."[18] She devotes much attention to nondiscursive symbolization and the compulsion to perform rites from "sheer inward need."[19] Langer reminds us that ritual preceded language as a form of symbolization and confirms the findings of others who conclude that man danced before he spoke. The solemn and significant activity of ritual emerged as gestures, not merely self-expressive, but expressive of right attitudes, of a celebrated deed held sacred, of a reality not otherwise expressible.

Thus the new insights into ritual provided fertile ground for the use of dance rites in modern art: they not only offered a new mode for ordering a perception of experience, but also revealed a more sensitive understanding of man. Psychological insights led to a new interpretation of man's basic need to dance; the study of dance as a *cultural* phenomenon resulted in an awareness of dance's broader sociological context.*

The poets whose work I examine were extremely sensitive to the reverberations of meaning in myth and ritual. Their personal experiences revealed in letters, essays, conversations, and finally revealed in the poetry itself provide evidence of their *conscious* awareness of the potentiality of these forms. They saw themselves, sometimes seriously, sometimes wittily, as twentieth-century shamans dancing order out of chaos. They knew the dancers and the dance and heralded their triumphs with unusual enthusiasm and empathy.

The Inspiration of Isadora

It was Isadora Duncan who first declared extravagantly, "I see America dancing!" Isadora exploded on the European

*It should be noted that such interest has hardly flagged recently. The impact of the social sciences on the study of dance and ritual is only beginning to be felt. Reporting on the Fourth Committee on Research in Dance (CORD) Conference in October 1974, Judith Lynne Hanna emphasized the broad scope of research by dance anthropologists. In "attempts to understand humans through dance" the conference grappled with epistemological and methodological issues. Debate centered on definitions of dance, phenomenological (ethnographic) versus analytic (structural) approaches, and the relationship between dance and other sociocultural phenomena.[20]

scene in 1900 with freedom and defiance combined with considerable talent and charismatic beauty. For two decades—in Paris, Vienna, London, and St. Petersburg—audiences sat in rapt wonder as the lustrous Isadora brought them her own creation of the dance. To the viewers of the late nineties, she was a welcome change from the stultifying atmosphere of the formal ballet from which all sense of "felt life" seemed absent. As the new century approached, new voices began to call for change in all the arts, and Isadora's was one of the first. For all the dancers after her she raised the banner of rebellion, questioning and rejecting what ballet had become and opening the way for the creation of a new genre. She was joined by Mary Wigman, Ruth St. Denis, Michel Fokine, and Martha Graham—all of whom provided the impetus to modern dance as we see it performed today.

She was born in 1878 in San Francisco and all her life spoke of the inspiration furnished by her California home—its pounding Pacific, its waving pine forests, the openness and freedom of the then unexploited West. Though her models were Greek, her dance was a thoroughly native product. Rejecting the ballet schools then training young girls to be frozen coquettes with technical expertise, Isadora scoffed at the imitation of decadent French ballet currently perpetuated in the Russian school. She insisted on going back to the model of the Greek *choros*, interpreting their art as more fluid, simpler, and less constrained. Dancing barefooted in loose Greek tunic, Isadora, as Curt Sachs recalls, "breathed life into the statues of the Greeks. She frees the old Hellenic dance from its rigidity of sculpture, from its sleep in the museums."[21] In essence, Isadora rediscovered the human body and offered new obeisance to its natural splendor. In rejecting the theatrical, the angular, the formalism of ballet, Isadora's dance was largely imageless, her style best described as lyrical. Though inspired by the music of Gluck, Wagner, and Tchaikovsky, she did not seek to interpret or visualize their music but instead received her personal inspiration from them. Her dance was an attempt to draw the relation between her inner emotions and the dancer's mode of expression. Viewers recall Isadora as a kind of "glorious, bounding Minerva"; her dance was an interesting admixture of classical Greek purity and uninhibited sexuality. She believed, as she wrote, that "spiritual expression must flow into the channels of the body, filling it with vibrating light," but she believed equally that the rules and restraints of an outmoded Victorian prudery must be stormed and overturned. This new dance, she wrote, "will be clean. I see America dancing, standing on one foot poised on the highest point of the Rockies her hands stretched out from the Atlantic to the Pacific, her fine head tossed to the sky, her forehead shining with a crown of a million stars."[22]

Throughout her short, meteoric career, her tastes were catholic. Her search for acceptance took her for her first triumphs to Europe: Budapest in 1903, Berlin in 1904, St. Petersburg in 1905, London in 1908. To these distant places she brought her own American dance (in the guise of a Greek revival!) born of the woods and the sea and the eternal spring of California, movements free as the form and organic structure of the body would allow, natural movements to affirm nature and deny artifice.

Her insistence on the interdependence of the arts—dance, music, sculpture, and poetry—shaped her own special articulation of movement and gesture. In 1922, her liaison and later marriage with Sergei Essenine, an Imagist poet, reinforced that awareness. Through Essenine, she met the poets Anatoly Mariengof, Vadim Shershenevich, and Ryurik Ivnov, but her friends had always numbered among them poets and writers. Now Essenine made her conscious of the new Imagist movement so that, teaching Russian children to dance, she would write: "I would take . . . the poem and teach the child to dance it in gesture and emotional translation of movement, and I would have the pleasure of seeing the face of the child light up with understanding, and would

16

know that he had actually learned through the movement of this poem what he was quite incapable of understanding from the words."[23] On another occasion, writing about the dance in the Greek *Choros*, she observed that the highest aim of dancing was to take its legitimate place in tragedy with music and poetry, to be the intermediary between the tragedy and the audience, creating harmony between them.

Isadora's vision was Whitmanesque: she saw her art as an integral exponent of the American myth, and her contemplation of the interacting arts testifies to the breadth of that vision. But a Duncan school of the dance was never permanently initiated nor did Isadora refine her theories of dance. Like Whitman's, her contribution lay in her rejection of the immediate past with its dead wood and ugliness. Like the prophet of poetry, she was the first priestess of the new art. Pound's tribute to Whitman best describes Isadora's own relation to her followers:

> It was you that broke the new wood,
> Now is a time for carving.

Among her own contemporaries that carving had already begun. Before Isadora could see the fruits of the revolution she had begun in Europe and carried home on numerous occasions with only limited success, her life was cut short in a tragic accident in France in 1927.

After Isadora

Following Isadora Duncan's flamboyant conquest of Europe's capitals, new developments began to be noted in the emerging dance of Germany and the United States. Mary Wigman reflected the influence of Isadora in the dance that grew out of ecstasy and went further in her recreation of primitive sources. Form was taken several steps beyond Isadora's personal, expressive dance, and a new preoccupation with space emerged. Wigman, introspective, philosophical, preoccupied with death and limitation, was important in broadening the symbolic implications of modern dance. In Wigman's art, as well as that of Rudolph Van Laban in Germany and Ruth St. Denis in America, theories of dance emerged that were to become the true foundations for the new genre. Dipping into American myth and ritual, St. Denis, as well as Martha Graham, Doris Humphrey, and Charles Weidman who followed—a whole generation of dancers—built on Isadora's fragile beginnings. The emphasis remained on improvisation, on an art based on the American idea and ideal while no less precise and perfect in execution than ballet. Modern dance took uncharted paths, as modern poetry was also to do. Both arts had come into being in a turbulent period of transition. Both shared a distaste for obvious expression and sought their essence in the elusive, evanescent, and indefinable moment. Both attempted to synthesize in a flash all the diverse and antithetic experiences of the new age. That modern dancers reflected the themes of modern poetry was no accident. They danced the patterns of nature and man's place in that pattern. They danced the human will as it exerted itself against hostile forces. They celebrated the earth, the human body, the fertility of all life. They performed the primitive rituals of earlier celebrants, testifying to their closeness to "reality." They pictured in dance form the mind of the city-dweller and the impact of the machine age on man. Modern dancers and the poets we shall examine took encouragement from each other's achievements, so that Hart Crane could applaud Portapovitch's great leap as his own imagination vaulted the "chained bay waters."

> Vault on the opal carpet of the sun,
> Barbaric Prince Igor;—or, blind Pierrot,
> Despair until the moon by tears be won:—
> Or, Daphnis, move among the bees with Chloe.

The Literary Backdrop

The literary forces that shaped the imagination of Eliot, Crane, Roethke, and Williams were congenial, as well, to the cultivation of dance images. Whether on the banks of the Thames, the Seine, or the Hudson, poets pondered the problem of creating a poetry that would dramatize the plight of the alienated artist in society; that would express the discontinuity that left him fragmented and rootless, yet still searching for something to affirm. Foremost, the poets were absorbed by the challenge of language, the words that "strain/Crack and sometimes break under the burden." They speculated on the possibility that the image, containing its own reality with a value beyond itself, as Baudelaire had believed, might indeed be ballast for a whole complex of thoughts and emotions. Imagism, in Pound's hands, was an attempt to codify what poets like Eliot had been intent upon for a decade: to produce language of greater precision, economy, and integrity than had appeared in the fin-de-siècle writing of the aesthetes. This quest for hard, oracular, concise symbols and images led the twentieth-century poets to penetrate the depths of their whole experience. They used old myths and sought untapped ones. As Yeats had delved into the Celtic past, the Irish conflict, Japanese Noh drama, and the world of mysticism to weave new mythologies, so Pound brought Japanese Haiku and the Provençal world of Bertran de Born into confrontation with the realities of world war and the tragedy of the poet: "A man with no fortune and with a name to come."

The question that interests me here is the degree to which the multimovements—Symbolism, Imagism, Vorticism—provided the poets whose work I examine with a stimulus for the increased use of dynamic images such as dance. Joseph Frank, in his essay "Spatial Form in Modern Literature," offers the most suitable context for seeking the answer. In tracing the modern writer's predilection to break out of traditional, prescribed laws of esthetic perception—namely, that form in the plastic arts is necessarily spatial while literature "makes use of language, composed of a succession of words proceeding through time," necessarily narrative—Frank has revealed the most crucial area of commonality in what he calls "the evolution of form in modern poetry." In fact, Frank points out, "modern literature exemplified by such writers as T. S. Eliot, Ezra Pound, Marcel Proust, and James Joyce, is moving in the direction of spatial form. This means that the reader is intended to apprehend their work, spatially, in a moment in time, rather than as a sequence." Frank points to Pound's definition of Imagism* not as a "pictorial reproduction, but as the unification of disparate ideas and emotions into a complex presented spatially."[25] Pound was to take the definition one step further to relieve the image of any static quality, rather to reveal an energy of its own: "The image is not an idea. It is a radiant node or cluster; it is . . . a VORTEX, from which and through which, and into which ideas are constantly rushing."[26] Hugh Kenner reinforced Pound's concept of the dynamic image when he wrote: "Imagism is energy . . . effort."[27] As the point of maximum energy, the image could transcend the fragmentation resulting from the spatialization of form in the poem; it could, through its infinite potentiality for transformation, become the chief means for unifying, for harmonizing, for synthesizing the experience of the poem. Recalling the mythic view that the flux that is chaos is man's enemy, we can concede the value of the poet's goal, as Frank views it, to "overcome . . . the time-elements involved in its perception and to reach toward some timeless dimension, free of historical limits, free indeed of the restraints of language itself."[28] It is not surprising, therefore, that poets would seize upon an image of dynamic motion, the dance, at once patterned by time and space but transcending

---

*Pound had defined the Image as "that which presents an intellectual and emotional complex in an instant of time."[24]

both, as a fitting metaphor for the experience of poetry. The dance was not an unfamiliar motif; poets and artists of the late nineteenth century—Symons, Gautier, Moreau, Heine, Huysmans, and Wilde, among others—reflected a sensitivity to the dance. By 1916 D. H. Lawrence had made the image his own metaphor for significant human activity and the greatest literary models in England and America, Yeats and Whitman, had written a poetry that literally danced its measures.

"How can we know the dancer from the dance?": William Butler Yeats

Frank Kermode's excellent study of Yeats's dancer has dramatized the remarkable impact of Romantic and Symbolist thought on a poet whose lifelong goal was to fuse the irreconcilable elements of his experience into a single image. Yeats had written "Hammer your thoughts into unity." The dance would be a "radiant truth,"[29] mythopoeic, a symbol of perfection, uniting body and soul, motion and stillness, time and timelessness. "The dancer is one of Yeats' great reconciling images," Kermode writes.[30] In "The Double Vision of Michael Robartes," she appears in his dream, dancing order into being in his disordered world. For the poetic Robartes, she is not only beauty incarnate and universal harmony manifested; she *is* the artist. Therein lay the poignant appeal of the dance for Yeats; like the dancer, he too could affirm the creative impulse embodied in patterned movements. "The Image is to be all movement, yet with a kind of stillness. She lacks separate intellectual content, her meanings, as the intellect receives them, must constantly be changing. She has the impassive, characterless face of Salome, so that there is nothing but the dance, and she and the dance are inconceivable apart, indivisible as body and soul, meaning and form, ought to be."[31] As Kermode describes her, she calls up the dancing god, a modern female Siva with the face of Salome, testifying that art is neither intellectual nor emotional but a perfect fusion of both.

In a study of the evolution of the dance in Yeats's poetry, Clinton Vickers[32] documents the presence of dance imagery in Yeats's work from the juvenilia to the Oisin poems and throughout the mature poetry. Early in Yeats, the image of the innocent child dancing on the wind conjures up an activity of joy amid the sorrows and tragedy of life:

> Dance there upon the shore
> What need have you to care
> For wind or water's roar?

But the aloofness of innocence becomes the detachment of transcendence in the Robartes poem as the dancer on the Rock of Cashel achieves a perfect stasis:

> O little did they care who danced between,
> And little she by whom her dance was seen
> So she had outdanced thought.
> Body perfection brought.

As the image becomes more complex, accruing in meaning from a childlike celebration to the mystical significance of ritual and ceremony, the pattern of the dance is related to a "threshold experience," a dance of death and purgation of the spirit. By the time of the Byzantium poems, the purgatorial nature of the dance appears to become the objective correlative for a religious as well as a psychic experience, what Kermode had called the inward-looking countenance. As Yeats himself had written, commenting upon Blake's poetry: "Dancing is the motion of desire in the lower or mortal world, as howling is its symbol,"[33] citing David's dancing before the ark and Urizen's on the mountain when infected and mad. As dancing in the Byzantium poems becomes the means of losing oneself to find oneself, the soul's need to abandon distinctions in order to reach God, we realize the complex nature of Yeats's dance:

> Dying into a dance,
> An agony of trance,
> . . . .
> Marbles of the dancing floor
> Break bitter furies of complexity.

But dance in Yeats was also an affirmation of life itself, as Crazy Jane emphasizes:

> God be with the times when I
> Cared not a thraneen for what chanced
> So that I had limbs to try
> Such a dance as there was danced—
> *Love is like the lion's tooth.*

Thus, throughout Yeats's poetry, the image of the dance often comes to symbolize the duality in the mind of the modern poet for whom antithesis was the very nature of existence: affirming life while searching for apotheosis; committing himself to art and an examination of the inner life, but like Crazy Jane, groveling in the "rag-and-bone shop of the heart," seeking in the ritual of dance a place where the natural and supernatural conjoin. In those early years of the new century, Yeats had sought what Roethke, Eliot, and Crane would seek in their own poetic journeys: the perfect image of reconciliation in a world of polarities, change, and disunity. Much later, a young American poet would write:

> I take this cadence from a man named Yeats;
> I take it, and I give it back again:
> . . . .
> Yes, I was dancing-mad, and how
> That came to be the bears and Yeats would know.

In those same early years, Isadora Duncan was reminding American poets of their literary heritage and of the "bridge," in Hart Crane's terms, between poetry and the dance. "The supreme poet of our country is Walt Whitman. I am indeed the spiritual daughter of Walt Whitman. For the children of America I will create a new dance that will express America."[34] Isadora proclaimed a truth that literary critics have supported *since* Eliot and Pound: Modern American poetry begins indeed with Whitman.* Despite the crosscurrents of literary vogues that attracted poets of the early decades of the century to *Symbolisme*, to English metaphysical poetry, to the lyrical tradition of *Provençale* troubadours, and to the *dolce stil nuovo* of Dante, and led them to create and abort such "movements" as Imagism, Vorticism, Cubism, and Futurism in poetry, the Whitman tradition shaped enduringly, and in fact accounted for, the continuity of American poetry. Reluctantly, Pound acknowledged that debt:

> I made a pact with you, Walt Whitman
> I have detested you long enough.
> I come to you as a grown child
> Who has had a pig-headed father;
> I am old enough now to make friends.
> It was you that broke the new wood,
> Now is the time for carving.
> We have one sap and one root—
> Let there be commerce between us.

Perhaps the twin impulses—continental and American—were possible because of a lack of conflict in poetic practice between the models. As Allen and Davis have amply demonstrated, the striking correspondences between Whitman's vision and that of the French Symbolists permitted their coexistence in the American poetic imagination.[36]

---

*In William Carlos Williams's observation, Whitman's free verse was "an assault on the very citadel of the poem itself."[35]

Most contemporary critics have come to believe that despite the rich contributions of the European tradition, the theme of modern American poetry—the American experience—and its language, form, and symbol found their inspiration in the poetry of Walt Whitman.

The question before us is the degree to which the Whitmanesque mode contributed to the choice of the dance as a significant image for modern poetry. We have already seen that the simultaneous emergence of modern dance and modern poetry, the impact of European models especially in the practice of Yeats, the innovative developments in the visual arts, and the growing importance of the mythical method with its accompanying reconsideration of myth and ritual all helped to shape a modern sensitivity to dance as a meaningful image. Did Whitman play a role in this growing consciousness? It is interesting that except for Eliot (who disdained Whitman yet reflected Whitman's fine sense of the inner form of poetry!), most American poets of the dance are enthusiastic in their homage to Whitman. Hart Crane made the "master singer" the subject of "Cape Hatteras":

> Our Meistersinger, thou set breath to steel;
> And it was thou who on the boldest heel
> Stood up and flung the span on even wing
> Of that great Bridge, our Myth, whereof I sing!

"My hand/in yours, Walt Whitman—/so—": Walt Whitman

To Walt Whitman, music and poetry were often interchangeable, and the added presence of cadenced measures testifies to his personal attachment to music and affection for the dance. Gay Wilson Allen notes that by 1842 Whitman was already a great devotee of the opera and folk music.[37] Joseph J. Rubin traces Whitman's passion for music, which led him inevitably to the "procession of European virtuosi and native choristers, in opera by Bellini, Rossini, and Donizetti" while working for *The Brooklyn Eagle.* In New Orleans, Whitman attended the operas presented there by the Paris Conservatory. He participated in soirées at Tammany and Tivoli where dancing was fast becoming the social pastime of the day. Rubin writes, "He may have felt too heavy to dance gracefully, for his six-foot frame carried nearly two hundred pounds. But he violated his own precept one July night. . . . He waltzed, did polkas, quadrilles, and Virginia reels until four in the morning."[38] His amusement at possessing neither grace "nor delicatesse, I cannot beguile the time with talk,/Awkward in the parlor, neither a dancer nor elegant," reminds us of Roethke's own rueful recollections of his clumsiness. But in a passage from "Letters from a Travelling Bachelor," Whitman gives us an account of the "strange doings" at Montauk where he rambled the cliffs with friends:

> Then we pranced forth again, like mad kine—we threw our hats in the air—aimed stones at the shrieking sea-gulls, mocked the wind, and imitated the cries of various animals in a style that beat nature all out! . . . We indulged in some impromptu quadrilles, of which the "chasez" took each participant couple so far away from the other that they were like never to get back. We hopped like crows; we pivoted like Indian dervishes; we went through the trial dance of *La Bayadere* with wonderful vigor.

As a spectator, Whitman enjoyed the dance, and was probably part of the admiring throng that greeted the ballerina Fanny Elssler on her several appearances in New York. Rubin describes the crowd that "cheered Fanny Elssler, filled her purse, and covered the stage with flowers in fifteen nights of Polish dances, and the La Tarantual [*sic*] and La Sylphide ballets. Some of the press, shocked by a dress slit at the thigh, branded her 'a gilded, glittering, shameless creature.' " For Whitman "imagination interpreted with simplicity and boldness was the nerve in the fingers of art." Gay Wilson Allen tells us that "Whitman championed the nude in art because he thought the human body 'the most beautiful organization of earth, exponent and minister of the highest being we immediately know.' "[39] Whitman would have delighted in Elssler just as he might one day have stood with the young Hart Crane and applauded Isadora!* Whitman had seen native American dancing, as we know from his comments on the performances of Dane Rice. At first he bemoaned Rice's singing and dancing as a cruel casting of Rice "to play a Negro," but later commended Rice for popularizing the "jigs, hornpipes, double cuts, double shuffles" and other dances as genuine folk art. That he had some modest knowledge of the native dances of foreign cultures is revealed in the passage celebrating dance worldwide in *Leaves of Grass:*

I hear the dance-music of all nations,
The waltz, some delicious measure, lapsing, bathing me in
    bliss,
The bolero to tinkling guitars and clattering castenets.

I see religious dances old and new,
I hear the sound of the Hebrew lyre,
I see the crusaders marching bearing the cross on high, to
    the martial clang of cymbals,
I hear dervishes monotonously chanting, interspers'd with
    frantic shouts, as they spin around turning always toward
    Mecca.
I see the rapt religious dances of the Persians and the Arabs,
Again, at Eleusis, home of Ceres, I see the modern Greeks
    dancing,
I hear them clapping their hands as they bend their bodies,
I hear the metrical shuffling of their feet.

---

*One of the few known "teachers" Isadora Duncan acknowledged, Ketti Lanner, had been a pupil in her youth in Vienna of Fanny Elssler—one of those intriguing threads woven into the story of modern dance! See Macdougall, *Isadora*.[40]

I see again the wild old Corybantian dance, the performers
  wounding each other,
I see the Roman youth to the shrill sound of flageolets
  throwing and catching their weapons,
As they fall on their knees and rise again.
. . . .
Fill me with all the voices of the universe.
Endow me with their throbbings, Nature's also,
The tempests, waters, winds, operas and chants, marches
  and dances.

Mere cataloguing apart, however, dance provided Whitman on many occasions with an artistic equation for his own sense of "process." As we examine all of his poetry, its outstanding quality is a vigorousness, a tensile strength, that we have come to associate with poetry of dynamic motion, in Whitman's own words: "electric, fresh, lusty." Whitman's great lyrical power does not obscure the sheer physical *presence* in his poetry. He wrote, when old and weakened, that a man "is a god walking the earth. The play of the body in motion takes a previously unknown grace. Merely to *move* is then a happiness, a pleasure." Whether splashing his bare feet on Paumanok's sands, or flying "those flights of a fluid and swallowing soul," or "speeding through space, speeding through heaven and the stars," Whitman's spirit moves "in measure" as he travels through America and beyond.

The image of the dance takes on symbolic nuances when he celebrates himself and the universe of natural objects. He perceives the inexorable motion of the "kosmos" as ceaseless float: "To me the converging objects of the universe perpetually flow," and he feels "the long pulsation, ebb and flow of endless motion." He is one who "walks with the tender and growing night," the "revolving cycles" themselves sweeping him round again. In another vision of dancing spheres, he reminds himself

Of the interminable sisters,
Of the ceaseless cotillions of sisters,
Of the centripetal and centrifugal sisters, the eldest and the
    younger sisters,
The beautiful sister we know dances on with the rest.

As the planets revolve, so too the sun *around us;* the images
of harmony in the macrocosm reflecting on the earth itself:
"The very sun swings itself and its systems around us,/Its
sun, and its again, all swing around us." So the mythic dance
of the celestial bodies—text for a multitude of Renaissance
lyrics—is adapted by Whitman to document the *wholeness* of
America's diverse and divided self. As Whitman had written
in the Preface to *Leaves of Grass*, "The poets of the kosmos
advance through all interpositions and coverings and tur-
moils and stratagems to first principles." He would give us a
vision and a man "cohered out of the tumult and chaos."
Even the divided continents would be joined like paired-off
dancers: "Europe to Asia, Africa join'd, and they to the New
World,/The lands, geographies, dancing before you, holding
a festival garland,/As brides and bridegrooms hand in hand."
    Joy and bounty are often expressed by Whitman in dancing:

O to have life henceforth a poem of new joys!
To dance, clap hands, exult, shout, skip, leap, roll on, float
    on!

Dance is a rite of initiation—whether sexual union, marriage,
or war. The erotic celebration of the flesh that will become
familiar in the poetry of Hart Crane and Theodore Roethke
have their origin in Whitman:

I am for those who believe in loose delights, I share the
    midnight orgies of young men,
I dance with the dancers and drink with the drinkers.

And celebrating the self, "I am satisfied—I see, dance, laugh, sing," becomes correspondingly a celebration of the whole cycle of life and death. In "The Sleepers," Whitman's most moving dance poem, the sequence is a rite of transcendence. The dreamer "wanders," then "stepping with light feet, swiftly and noiselessly stepping and stopping," he journeys into the dream-world of the "others":

And I become the other dreamers,
I am a dance—play up there! the fit is whirling me fast!

It is the dance that unites him with the others, and he names the sleepers in a Whitmanesque catalogue of infinite diversity: "The laugher and the weeper, the dancer, the midnight widow, the red squaw," and swears "they are all beautiful." The images of flowing and uniting that distinguish "The Sleepers" are those of harmonizing process.

Again, in "When Lilacs Last in the Dooryard Bloomed," the hermit thrush, welcoming approaching death, fuses the images of song, dance, and poetry in the mediating vision of the artist who perceives all death as a promise of rebirth:

Dark mother always gliding near with soft feet,
Have none chanted for thee a chant of fullest welcome?
Then I chant it for thee, I glorify thee above all,
I bring thee a song that when thou must indeed come, come
    unfalteringly.
. . . .

For me to the glad serenades,
Dances for thee I propose saluting thee, adornments and
    feastings for thee,
And the sights of the open landscape and the high-spread sky
    are fitting,
And life and the fields, and the huge and thoughtful night.

Late in his life, Walt Whitman celebrated both his country's centennial, 1876, and his own faith in the brotherhood of all men in a poem that itself is the image of a dance. It is reproduced here, not only because it is one of Whitman's lesser-known poems, but because the "round" he dances is revealed in the unusual rhyme and meter:

Hands Round

See! see! where the sun is beaming!
See! see! see! all the bright stars, gleaming!
See by day how the sun is beaming
See by night all the far stars gleaming
What the charm of Power unbroken?
What the spell of ceaseless token?
O its hand in hand, & a Union of all
What Columbia's? friendliest token?
'Tis the hands we take for the Union of all
Here's mine—give me thine—for the Union of all
What Columbia's friendliest token?
All hands round for the Union all!
Here's mine—give me thine—for the Union all

Stars up above in eternal lustre
Stars of the States in a compact clustre
Clasping, holding, earthward, heavenward
Circling, moving, roundward & onward
All hands round for the Union all
Here's mine—give me thine—for the Union all
Red, white, blue, to the westward
Red, white, blue, with the breezes waving
All combining, folding, loving,

Northward, Southward, Westward moving
O its all hands round for the Union all
Here's mine—give me thine—for the Union all
Clasping, circling, earthward, heavenward!
Onward! onward! onward! onward!
Stars for the sky in an eternal lustre
Stars for the earth in a compact clustre

31

Then our hands here we give for the Union all!
O its all hand round—and each for all!

In a last poetic fragment, only recently published, Whitman again spoke in the language of the "round":

Advancing, retreating, and hand in hand
Duly with rhythmic steps turning and mouths to the right or
the left reverting,
You chorus of brothers, and sisters
Moving forever round the circles of the earth

Although it is difficult to measure the degree of indebtedness of one generation of poets to another, and apart from the testimony of Pound and Crane—"Thy wand/Has beat a song, O Walt,—there and beyond!"—the dance figures importantly in American poetry from Whitman's time to our own. The poetic images of dance and dancer recur in endless variety in the poetry of Eliot, Crane, Roethke, and Williams. Each seemed aware of the potentiality of dance to express, as Susanne Langer observed, "the verbally ineffable yet inexpressible law of vital experience."[41] The American poet often "sang his didn't and danced his did," in e. e. cummings's words—choosing patterns of dance images that reflected his own vision of modern life and the "undiscovered continent" within.

NOTES

1. Nikos Kazantzakis, *Report to Greco* (New York: Bantam, 1961), pp. 143–44.
2. Langer, "The Dynamic Image," in *Problems in Art*, 1951, p. 7.
3. Williams, *Autobiography*, 1948, p. 373.
4. Selden, *The Dancer's Quest*, 1935, p. 15.
5. Hart Crane, Letter to Gorham Munson, 1922, in Unterecker, *Voyager*, 1969, p. 265.

6. Lloyd, *The Borzoi Book of Modern Dance*, 1949, p. 3.

7. Duncan, *My Life*, 1927, p. 31.

8. Lloyd, p. xx.

9. Ezra Pound quoted by Eliot, "Ezra Pound: His Metric and His Poetry," in *To Criticize the Critic*, 1965, p. 171.

10. Lloyd, p. xx.

11. Graves, *The Greek Myths*, vol. II, 1955, p. 146.

12. See Spears, *Dionysus and the City*, 1970.

13. Sanders, Nelson, and Rosenthal, eds., Introduction, 1970, p. 1.

14. Kermode, *Romantic Image*, 1957.

15. Jean Erdman, "The Dance as Non-Verbal Image," in *The Dance Has Many Faces*, ed. Sorell, 1951, p. 199.

16. Nietzsche, *The Birth of Tragedy*, 1956, pp. 36–37.

17. Ernst Cassirer, *The Philosophy of Symbolic Forms:* vol. II, *Mythical Thought*, tr. Ralph Manheim (New Haven: Yale University Press, 1955), p. 39.

18. Susanne K. Langer, *Philosophy in a New Key* (New York: Mentor, 1951), p. 52.

19. Ibid., p. 116.

20. Judith Lynne Hanna, "The Anthropology of Dance: Reflections on the CORD Conference," *Current Anthropology* 16, no. 3 (September 1975).

21. Sachs, *World History of the Dance*, 1952, p. 447.

22. Isadora Duncan, "Two Rebels, Two Giants: Isadora and Martha," in *The Dance Has Many Faces*, p. 170.

23. Isadora Duncan, "Dancing in Relation to Religion and Love," *Theatre Arts Monthly* 11 (August 1927), p. 389.

24. Ezra Pound, *The Literary Essays of Ezra Pound* (New York: New Directions, 1954), p. 4.

25. Joseph Frank, "Spatial Form in Modern Literature," in *Criticism, The Foundations of Modern Literary Judgment*, eds. Schorer, Miles, and McKenzie, 1948, pp. 379–92.

26. Pound, "Vorticism," in *Gaudier-Brzeska*, 1917, p. 92.

27. Kenner, *The Pound Era*, 1971, p. 186.

28. Frank, p. 391.

29. Kermode, p. 2.

30. Ibid., p. 48.

31. Ibid., p. 85.

32. Vickers, "Image and Symbol," 1974.

33. W. B. Yeats, *Blake* (London: B. Quaritch, 1893), p. 402.

34. Duncan, *My Life*, p. 31.

35. William Carlos Williams, "An Essay on *Leaves of Grass*," in Walt Whitman, *Leaves of Grass* (New York: W. W. Norton, 1973), p. 903.

36. Allen and Davis, *Walt Whitman's Poems*, 1955, Introduction, pp. 1–51.

37. Gay Wilson Allen, *The Solitary Singer* (New York: Macmillan, 1955), p. 50.

38. These and following observations in Joseph J. Rubin, *The Historic Whitman* (University Park: Pennsylvania State University Press, 1973).

39. Allen, p. 109.

40. Allan Ross MacDougall, *Isadora*, 1960.

41. Langer, p. 217.

CHAPTER II

Follow the Dance: T. S. Eliot

... it is ultimately the function of art, in imposing a credible order upon ordinary reality, and thereby eliciting some perception of an order in reality, to bring us to a condition of serenity, stillness, and reconciliation.

—"Poetry and Drama"

"Instinct for the Dance—a caper part—" Emily Dickinson called that inclination to tune in to the universal rhythm of moving things. The dance as an image in T. S. Eliot's poetry might have its source, as well, in his own unconscious search for an experience beyond the "thousand deliberations of the mind." He would counsel his spirit in "East Coker" to "wait without thought, for you are not ready for thought:/So the darkness shall be the light and the stillness the dancing." The lines intervene in the "purgatorial" passage of the poem as the soul is urged to divest itself of worldly concerns and progress to the "faith and the love and the hope" awaiting the quester at the close of "Little Gidding." In this, his most complete poem of faith, *Four Quartets*, "light" and "dancing" become equated. The dance, a crucial human, godly, and cosmic activity often testifies to the true and immutable logos of the world without whose certain knowledge man is alienated, a wanderer. Dante's divine *light* becomes linked inextricably to the dance at the "still center of the turning world."

A fundamental tension in Eliot's poetry between the wisdom yielded up by the senses and by the operations of the intellect led him naturally to those "images of awareness" Leonard Unger has so well charted.¹ Eliot had mused on the mysterious roots of a poet's imagery in "The Use of Poetry and the Use of Criticism." They grow not only from what he reads, he points out, but "from the whole of his sensitive life since early childhood." Jung had examined this psychic phenomenon of the resonating imagination with equal wonder: "In addition to memories from a long-distant conscious past, completely new thoughts and creative ideas can also present themselves from the unconscious—thoughts and ideas that have never been conscious before."²

All of his life, Eliot's preoccupation with music afforded him a rich source for poetic images; his poetic structures often resemble musical arrangement. The abundant references to musical terms and the snatches of tunes only begin to suggest the sensitivity to music that pervades his poetry. He was to write:

> I believe that the properties in which music concerns the poet most nearly, are the sense of rhythm and the sense of structure. . . . There are possibilities for verse which bear some analogy to the development of a theme by different groups of instruments; there are possibilities of transitions in a poem comparable to the different movements of a symphony or a quartet; there are possibilities of contrapuntal arrangement of subject matter.³

Those critics concerned with the "music of poetry" in Eliot's forms and themes have amply noted the degree to which these analogies illuminate his verse.⁴ The dance as a *presence* in his poetry is equally significant, though we might speculate, like Eliot himself, on those sources in his unconscious. More factually, we know that Eliot had a lively interest in ballet all his life. He was married to a ballet dancer, knew several ballets expertly enough to review them for the *Criterion*, and admired not only the geniuses of the Ballet Russe, Vaslav Nijinsky and Diaghilev, but music-hall entertainers like Mistinguette.⁵

In addition, Eliot was fully conversant with the ongoing debates in the literature of sociology and anthropology concerning myths and rituals; he regularly reviewed books for the *International Journal of Ethics*, on one occasion, in fact, mediating an "argument" between Clement C. Webb and Lucien Lévy-Bruhl. Eliot's understanding of the role of dance rituals in primitive myth enhances our own appreciation of his use of the dance, especially in his later poetry.

To the extent that the dance in Eliot's poetry becomes a kind of divinely orchestrated rite—"still and still moving/into another intensity"—it would be useful to review briefly the role of dance in primitive ritual. The importance of rites in the self-contained world of myth cannot be overstressed. Enacted or danced, rites served a variety of functions but all acknowledged the indivisibility of man, nature, and the Cosmos, having their commonality in a sacred "beginning." Primitive dancers could, through the magic of dance, abolish time, identify with the god *ab origine*, commemorate the moment of origin, celebrate the cyclical order of the seasons, and ensure favorable results in daily life. Defying the disorder and temporality of the profane world, dance rites transformed the participants into the realm of the absolute and the eternal. So man could triumph over change and time. Whether in the guise of Osiris, Dionysus, Siva, or the Dancing Jesus, the shaman-gods of more highly developed cultures perpetuated the concept of a dancing deity. "We dance to free ourselves from the fear of life," dancer Joseph Gregor declared, lifting the curtain on a thousand years of dance history.[6] Eliot reflects these ancient associations of myth and ritual combined with the rebirth of ballet and dance in his own age, and his view of the "possibilities" of music could well be extended to its visual counterpart, the dance. He had already lauded Joyce for choosing the "mythical method": "It is simply a way of controlling, of ordering, of giving a shape and a significance to the immense panorama of futility and anarchy which is contemporary history."[7] He revered rite as the

"High Dream"[8] and his personal predilection for the dance and dancers of his age provided his fertile imagination with a dynamic and multifaceted image.

Thus Eliot's dance reflects with varying emphasis all the symbolic meanings accrued over a long history. In a mythic sense, dance images a sacred harmonizing faculty. In "Burnt Norton" Eliot tells us "there is only the dance," expressing the ineffable, transforming time and change into an imperishable pattern of movement. In Eliot's poetry, as in myth, dance harmonizes life and death, stillness and motion, form and spirit. Dance affirms for Eliot, as for Yeats, the creative impulse embodied in patterned movements—the power of the dancer Siva who "danced the world into being," and whose dance "kept it alive."[9] Simultaneously, dance becomes the symbol for the triumph of pure art, creating images Kermode notes that "are uniquely alive because of their participation in a higher order of existence."[10] Words themselves coalesce into a dynamic pattern of ends and beginnings: "The complete consort dancing together." In another sense in Eliot's poetry, dance is a significant ritual transforming and elevating human activity: the manifestation of the High Dream of pageant and splendor he sees in Dante's Earthly Paradise—a dream man seems to have lost in the modern world. Since dance marks the sacred seasons, man's and nature's, it offers an archetypal experience for recapturing the past, for its essential nature is communication beyond the threshold of consciousness. Dance would appear to be an expression for Eliot of the unified sensibility, externalizing in patterned movements states of feeling that are otherwise inexpressible. And dance would always suggest more than itself: an activity close in spirit to the elusive moments in the rose garden, sensed and only partially understood. "I can only say, there we have been: but I cannot say where."

As noted earlier, these multiple symbols have their antithesis in parody: a debased ritual. At times it is a *danse macabre* defined by Northrop Frye as "an ironic reversal of the kind of romanticism that we have in the serious visions of the other world,"[11] or the dance takes on the madness of Blake's Urizen dancing on the mountain. Even in Eliot's later poetry, at the precise moment when he seems to achieve his vision, he despairs of the realities, and his dance reinforces the observation in "The Dry Salvages": "We had the experience but missed the meaning." The simple peasants dancing in "East Coker" seem similarly "unenlightened" though they perform the rites of the seasonal cycle and maintain a kind of serious "necessarye coniunction." As we shall see, in the evolution of Eliot's poetry of the dance, the orchestration of these contrapuntal motifs provides a tension that dramatizes Eliot's dual vision and sets its ironic tone.

Eliot's wasteland poetry abounds in images of futile and degraded activity, but even there we find the *glimmering* presence of another kind of "dance," one that could elevate man and expiate his suffering. Thus An Invitation to the Dance in "A Cooking Egg" sits unheeded on the mantelpiece amid the bric-a-brac of the stifling modern world. Conversely, we are invited to celebrate the ordered rhythm perceived in the natural world of "Cape Ann," and to participate in the experience that will unite us with it:

> O the goldfinch at noon. . . .
> . . . . Follow the feet
> Of the walker, the water thrush. Follow the flight
> Of the dancing arrow, the purple martin. . . .
> . . . . Follow the dance

But characteristically the final line returns us to this world as the speaker mockingly poses his idle "palaver" against the music of the communing birds: the song sparrow, the Blackburnian warbler, the shrill-whistling quail. The balance of opposing tensions is best expressed in Prufrock's own entrapment in a time-locked, vacuous society even while he senses the possibility of escape to another dimension of reality. Woven into the monotonous round of meaningless actions, a sudden flash of truth that a hundred visions might reveal is as rapidly obliterated by the taking of a toast and tea. "Pinned and wriggling on the wall" in a kind of death dance, Prufrock is no David who "danced before the Lord with all his might," touched with a spark of the divine. An oblique reference to Salome's dance, "Though I have seen my head (grown slightly bald) brought in upon a platter," reminds us that Prufrock's suffering—contrasted with that of John the Baptist—is unmitigated by noble action. Only in a fleeting moment, dreaming of the mermaids, can Prufrock dare to envision another reality:

> I have seen them riding seaward on the waves
> Combing the white hair of the waves blown back
> When the wind blows the water white and black.

The lyrical quality of this final vision is the closest we come in the poem to the beneficence of ritual movement. The mermaids transcend time in a dream that possesses a balletic quality. They are themselves beyond human change. They celebrate the harmony of opposites in a rhythmic nature figured here in the "waters white and black"; the beauty of the "sea-girls wreathed in seaweed red and brown," singing "each to each" is a revelation of art. But as the human voices call Prufrock back, we anticipate Eliot's observation in "The Dry Salvages," that "to apprehend/the point of intersection of the timeless/With time, is an occupation for the saint."

So it is that the almost insane dance is sought as the agent of transfiguration in "The Death of Saint Narcissus." David Bernstein[12] has analyzed the poem as an outgrowth of Eliot's knowledge of the life and art of dancer Vaslav Nijinsky, whose meteoric rise in the ballet world of the early decades of the twentieth century and ultimate lapse into a permanent

40

catatonic state is a tragic chapter in the history of the dance. Bernstein sheds light on an early poem of little interest to critics formerly save for the first stanza, which Eliot borrowed for *The Waste Land*.* Bernstein reminds us of Nijinsky's presence in Paris in 1911 when Eliot, studying at the Sorbonne, must surely have attended performances of Diaghilev's Ballet Russe. Eliot's lifelong interest in ballet, his marriage to a dancer, his reviews of "Le Sacre du Printemps," and his presence in Switzerland shortly after the dancer's breakdown all suggest that Eliot was deeply moved by Nijinsky's tragic life. Eerie parallels in the poem to Nijinsky's diary (which Eliot could not have known) and the account of the spectacle "Marriage avec Dieu" which Nijinsky performed immediately before his fall into oblivion (an account Eliot could have known) point up, among other things, the identification Eliot made between dancer and saint. That Eliot probably attended Nijinsky's performance of Fokine's "Narcisse" (in 1911) provides the final thread in his weaving together of the themes of the poem and the dramatic events of Nijinsky's life. In the words of Nijinsky's wife, speaking of the "Marriage avec Dieu," it was "the dance of life against death." So too the underlying theme of the poem: an attempt at transformation and transcendence in the ritual of the dance as the Chosen One in "Le Sacre du Printemps" restores life to a barren wasteland.

The dance in the poem moves from the perfection of the dancer's art at the height of his powers to the twisting, convulsive motions of the artist who could not live in the world of men to the series of tortuous transformations to, finally, the

---

*Come under the shadow of this gray rock—
Come in under the shadow of this gray rock,
And I will show you something different from either
Your shadow sprawling over the sand at daybreak, or
Your shadow leaping behind the fire against the red rock;
I will show you his bloody cloth and limbs
And the gray shadow on his lips.

failure to transcend himself. The saint's final dance rite bespeaks the awesome terror of the attempt to reach God, to surrender to divine authority.

> So he became a dancer to God.
> Because his flesh was in love with the burning arrows
> He danced on the hot sand
> Until the arrows came.

Narcissus's dance is a reflection of the vulgarized gestures of the wasteland city as well as his own narcissistic self-worship; his union with God is thwarted by his inability to purify or transcend himself. The fleeting vision of a dancing shaman is followed by the human reality: Narcissus "green, dry and stained/With the shadow in his mouth," is insensate and entrapped. The sharp distinction between the spirit dancing toward God and the inanimate husk that remains points up the paradox of flesh and spirit that Nijinsky's own life symbolized. Apart from the interesting parallels with Nijinsky's career and personal spiritual crisis, the poem is of course absorbing as another illustration of an early Eliot attempt to relate dancing, here clearly ritualistic activity, to the process of transcendence. If the poem fails in its emotional and spiritual effects, it is perhaps because the poet had not yet achieved his own strategy for using the dance image. Later, in the *Four Quartets* and "The Hollow Men," Eliot would have a more distinctly defined set of correlatives for the positive and negative aspects of the dance. Eliot's own valuation of this early poem is evident by his omission of it in any of his collected verse. It was published posthumously, although Bernstein dates it as having been written between 1919 and 1922.

In the world of ordinary people—the world of "Portrait of a Lady"—the dance appears as a *debased* ritual against the rhythmic backdrop of seasonal change. The first hint comes in the discordant music in the speaker's brain, an ironic reversal of Chopin's Prelude:

> Among the windings of the violins
> And the ariettes
> Of cracked corners
> Inside my brain a dull tom-tom begins
> Absurdly hammering a prelude of its own.

The music—a "false note," an insistent "out-of-tune," a "worn-out song"—is part of an image pattern that includes the Greek "murdered at a Polish dance," suggesting violation, vulgarity, and unnatural activity. These provide the prelude for the self-awareness finally experienced by the speaker. The real sense of his humiliation is imaged in the bestial forms:

> And I must borrow every changing shape
> To find expression . . . dance, dance
> Like a dancing bear,
> Cry like a parrot, chatter like an ape.

The passage recalls not only the familiar prancing bears at the circus whose parodies of men draw loud laughter, but ironically juxtaposes the bears of Shrovetide rituals.* The sense of futility that qualifies the experience in both passages increases the poignancy of the search: the parody of the dancing bear signals the failure in communication not only between men, or between man and the natural order of the cosmos, but between the experience and its expression. Thus the epiphany comes in the speaker's knowledge that "we are really in the dark." The motifs of surfeit and death that have informed the poem throughout:—"Among the smoke and fog of a December afternoon"—close round the final scene. The music "successful with a dying 'fall' " recalls Duke Orsino's melancholy request:

*For a fuller discussion of the dancing bear in myth and poetry see Chapter IV.

> If music be the food of love, play on,
> Give me excess of it, that surfeiting,
> The appetite may sicken, and so die.
> That strain again! It had a dying fall. . .

The final irony, already familiar in Eliot, is that the Duke's music of love is here the smiling speaker's music of death, "Now we talk of dying," that has come not so much from satiety as starvation! The final trail of unanswered questions poses again the tension provided in the dance image of communion on one hand and destruction and death on the other.

This polarity of symbols is again apparent in "Cousin Nancy" where Nancy Elicott's seemingly healthy and vigorous activity is clearly destructive. That Nancy "smoked/And danced all the modern dances" poses a disturbing paradox since to Eliot "modern" always suggested discontinuity and disinheritance. Yet in the stifled world of Boston, one can admire her youthful striding and riding over the barren New England hills. It would appear that the entire poem turns on the ambiguity of "modern dance"—all the contemporary world has to confront Emerson's "army of unalterable law."

In *The Waste Land*, a search that uncovers only lost or debased rituals, two negative images fulfill Eliot's black vision of the modern world. The first, the aimless activity of "crowds of people, walking round and round in a ring" (suggesting Dante's damned in the antechamber of Hell), although not a dance itself, prefigures the *danse macabre* of the Hollow Men: in one "each man fixed his eyes before his feet," while in the other, "the eyes are not here/There are no eyes here . . . In this last of meeting places/We grope together." The despair in *The Waste Land* emanates from the failure to unite oneself with a lifegiving activity—the circling crowd a bitter parody of the early ring dances connoting wholeness and continuity in nature. The second, the evocation of the children singing in the cupola, contrasts sharply with the dissolution of the Unreal City symbolized in "London Bridge is falling down falling down," a ring dance marking death. This contrapuntal motif persists in Eliot's poetry. The emblem of discordance, the enemy of pattern, continues to threaten in "Burnt Norton":

> ... The Word in the desert
> Is most attacked by voices of temptation
> The crying shadow in the funeral dance,
> The loud lament of the disconsolate chimera.

The affirmation ultimately articulated in "Burnt Norton," "The detail of the pattern is movement," is suggested less confidently in *The Waste Land*, barely whispered in the fragment from another purification rite, Arnaut Daniel's:

> Poi s'ascose nel foco che gli affina.
> (Then he threw himself into the refining fire.)

That Eliot perceived Daniel's rite as a dance is echoed in the *Four Quartets:* "Unless restored by that refining fire/Where you must move in measure like a dancer."

In "The Hollow Men" we are beyond despair. The multiple associations evoked by the sightless circling figures merge in the single image:

> Here we go round the prickly pear
> Prickly pear prickly pear
> Here we go round the prickly pear
> At five o'clock in the morning.

On one level, the debased "dance" of the Hollow Men is an ironic counterpart of the ritual celebration of Guy Fawkes, danced yearly around a blazing bonfire, connoting the vitality of a now legendary figure who dared unite "the idea and the reality, the motion and the act." On another level, it parodies the voices of the children chiming "here we go round the mulberry bush,"[13] once perhaps a sacred rite of spring and renewal, its meaning now lost in a child's game. On yet another level, its insistent circling recalls the graveside dances of the past when the rites of death and transcendence were recognized:

> Ring around a Rosie (Rosalie)
> Pockets full of posies
> Ashes, ashes,
> All fall down.

> 'Tis for Rosalie they sing
> Alleluja
> She is done with sorrowing—
> So we dance and so we sing.[14]

The striking difference is that Rosalie is "done with sorrowing," while "This is the way the world ends . . ." testifies to the ultimate failure of the "hope only/Of empty men." The combined effect of the dance is a mood of hopelessness and horror that pervades Eliot's wasteland. As always in Eliot's poetry, the wrench comes with the awareness that the rituals are present but always vitiated. Thus death itself, recalling the snickering Footman in "Prufrock," is anticlimax:

> This is the way the world ends
> This is the way the world ends
> This is the way the world ends
> Not with a bang but a whimper.

The singsong finale carrying us back to the circling children and the Hollow Men turning round the prickly pear is the dance of death.

Ash-Wednesday is sometimes seen as a distinct turning point in Eliot's vision when he left the wasteland behind and set himself the task of a more fruitful search in the emblem of a purgatorial experience. An important precursor to the fullest expression of the dance in the *Four Quartets*, *Ash-Wednesday* develops its entire theme in the image of "turning." The whole poem is structured on a ritual: The Ash-Wednesday Sacrifice of the Mass and the ascent of Mt. Purgatory in Dante's *Commedia*, both symbolic acts of death and rebirth. Opening with the now-familiar litany:

> Because I do not hope to turn again
> Because I do not hope
> Because I do not hope to turn
> Desiring this man's gift and that man's scope . . .

the poem presents an image of the turning world, a *mandala* wheel whose circle images wholeness of being, a pattern of harmony and movement already associated with the dance. The circling motion which will be celebrated in "Burnt Norton" as the unity of the cosmos is heralded here in the manifold image of turning. Combining Dante's vision of the penitential turning round Mt. Purgatory with the Ash-Wednesday concept of turning away from the world and turning to God, Eliot has invested the image with the emotions of agony, conflict, surrender, and affirmation. Although the speaker in *Ash-Wednesday* achieves no more than an understanding of his own aspiration, limitation, and dependence on divine will, the possibility of a turning that can effect a union with "the spirit of the river, the spirit of the sea" is present and serves to strengthen his resolve. As elsewhere in Eliot's poetry, the restoration of hope comes with the intensity of beauty felt in the natural world,

> From the wide window toward the granite shore
> The white sails still fly seaward, seaward flying
> Unbroken wings . . .

and the pattern of movement, here in the prophecy to the wind, affirms the wholeness he wishes to share.

The epigraphs to the *Four Quartets*, which set the tone for the dance images that figure largely in "Burnt Norton," recur in "East Coker" and again in "Little Gidding." The fragments from Heraclitus proclaim the truths of the mythical view of reality and prefigure their celebration in each of the Quartets. The first asserts unity-in-diversity in the universe and the centrality of divine intelligence while the second affirms Heraclitus's observance of the circular nature of the universal pattern.

An understanding of the "Still Point" is essential both for its symbolic function in the *Four Quartets* and for its relation to the dance. We recall* that the mythical accent fixes the zone of sacred reality as distinguished from the profane, empirical world. Where they intersect, at the meeting point of Heaven and Earth, there is God, the sacred center of the universe. The characteristics of the Still Point are those that myth recognizes as absolute: the divine nature of its essence, unaffected by empirical time, space, motion, or change. Thomas Browne best reflected the essence of the Still Point when he observed, "His whole duration being one permanent point, without Succession, Parts, Flux, of Division."[16] At the Still Point lies the harmonizing faculty of divine intelligence that reconciles apparent opposites. In his discussion of the Still Point in Dante's *Commedia*, Charles Singleton suggests that we visualize "a vertical line, a line of ascent in time in the upward way to God. And let there be a horizontal line, as it were, drawn across the vertical line by a procession symbolizing time. Where these lines meet—there Beatrice comes—as Christ."[17] Where these lines meet in the *Four Quartets*—there is the Still Point intersecting time and timelessness. Ultimately, the route to the Still Point involves a return to origins, the Beginning, through a return to Chaos, or death, and then to rebirth. Though Heraclitus does not

*I have treated the mythic element in Eliot's poetry in "T. S. Eliot's 'Purgatorio': The Structure of *Ash-Wednesday*" and in "The Mythic Perspective of Eliot's 'The Dry Salvages.'"[15]

define a Still Center, he recognizes, nevertheless, a central harmony that transcends the apparently meaningless movements of the world.* The search for union with the Still Point is, then, the transcendent objective of the poem. The dance images the presence of that harmony intrinsic to the universe, and the recognition of the dance in the microcosm/ macrocosm is the quester's own achievement "in and out of time" of that union. In Kermode's discussion of Yeats's dancer, he appears almost to paraphrase "Burnt Norton": "The image is to be all movement yet with a kind of stillness. . . . She has the impassive, characterless face of Salome, so that there is nothing but the dance, and she and the dance are inconceivable apart, indivisible as body and soul, meaning and form, ought to be."[19]

The musical overture of "Burnt Norton" comes in the rose garden in "the unheard music hidden in the shrubbery," followed by motion; "So we moved, and they, in a formal pattern." The harmony of sense and spirit achieved by the dance is first observed in the microcosm, then the macrocosm:

> The trilling wire in the blood
> Sings below inveterate scars
> And reconciles forgotten wars.
> The dance along the artery
> The circulation of the lymph
> Are figured in the drift of stars
> Ascend to summer in the tree
> We move about the moving tree
> In light upon the figured leaf
> And hear upon the sodden floor
> Below, the boarhound and the boar
> Pursue their patterns as before
> But reconciled among the stars.

*"The lovely dancing lyric . . . is obviously based on the Heraclitean idea of the perpetual strife which resolves itself into beautiful harmony. . . . The still point can be approached only through paradox and negation."[18]

The natural rhythms of the biological process, the patterns of actions in the natural world, and the movement of the heavenly bodies are expressed in the dance that is itself an articulation of life. We might recall the words of the Dominican monk Raffaelo delle Columbe, who wrote in 1622, "The dance is a symbol of the universal order and can be compared with the dance of the stars. For prayer is a spiritual dance. . . . God leads inside the ring."[20] Conscious of the reconciliation "among the stars," the speaker then moves to his assertion of faith in the face of divine paradox:

At the still point of the turning world. Neither flesh nor
  fleshless;
Neither from nor towards; at the still point, there the dance
  is,
But neither arrest nor movement. And do not call it fixity,
Where past and future are gathered. Neither movement from
  nor towards,
Neither ascent nor decline. Except for the point, the still
  point,
There would be no dance, and there is only the dance.

Gathered into one image are all of Eliot's positive connotations of the dance: unifying, timeless, transcendent—the permanent and the beautiful. Later in "Burnt Norton" Eliot—wrestling with the burdens of language—repeats this idea:

> Only by the form, the pattern,
> Can words or music reach
> The stillness, as a Chinese jar still
> Moves perpetually in its stillness.

Thus in "Burnt Norton" mythic, religious, and artistic overtones merge in a singular image that is itself a unity of thought and expression. The assertion that "there we have been, but I cannot say where" does not diminish the experience but reinforces the persistence of a search for its repetition. The dance in "Burnt Norton" is one of Eliot's significant triumphs; he unites faith and poetic ideal in this one image of God incarnate in the dance, achieving an effect of great artistic intensity.

In "East Coker," the cyclical rhythms in nature and men's lives, echoing Ecclesiastes, introduce the vision that returns us to the world of Thomas Elyot in the sixteenth century. It is Midsummer Eve, traditional time of seasonal rites when the process in nature and human process are jointly celebrated in the sacramental "daunsinge." In the voice of Sir Thomas, the ritual is pictured:

> In that open field
> If you do not come too close, if you do not come too close,
> On a Summer midnight, you can hear the music
> Of the weak pipe and the little drum
> And see them dancing around a bonfire
> The association of man and woman
> In daunsinge, signifying matrimonie—
> A dignified and commodious sacrament.
> Two and two, necessarye coniunction,
> Holding eche other by the hand or the arm
> Whiche betokeneth concorde. Round and round the fire
> Leaping through the flames or joined in circles,
> Rustically solemn or in rustic laughter
> Lifting heavy feet in clumsy shoes,
> Earth feet, loam feet, lifted in country mirth
> Mirth of those long since under earth
> Nourishing the corn. Keeping time,
> Keeping the rhythm in their dancing
> As in their living in the living seasons . . .

The image of the harmonious dancing with its emphasis on dignity, conjunction, and concord, encloses within it as well the necessary life rhythms of birth, coupling, and death. The final words of the passage, "dung and death," are an inexorable reminder of man's destiny; and the dream of Sir Thomas, while reassuring man of his place in the cyclical pattern of nature, is insufficient without the uplifting vision of his union with God. Toward the end of "East Coker" the speaker, ruminating on his humanistic forefathers who "deceived us/Or deceived themselves," and observing the phenomenon of succession, echoes the theme of the *danse macabre:*

> The houses are all gone under the sea.
> The dancers are all gone under the hill.

He prepares himself for the "further union, deeper communion," not yet achieved. It could only come with the experience of St. John of the Cross in the dark night of the soul, and until then "the faith and the love and the hope are all in the waiting." Only then, "the darkness shall be the light, and the stillness the dancing." The image of the transcendent dance appears with greatest intensity in the final words:

> We must be still and still moving
> Into another intensity . . .

The motif of fire is orchestrated with great skill in "Little Gidding" and serves to illuminate an important use of the dance as ritual. Among its several connotations are the tragic and destructive fire that laid waste Nicholas Ferrar's shrine in 1625; the Pentecostal fire when the words of God were received by the disciples; the fire of Dante's Hell as well as the purifying fire of Arnaut Daniel's sacrifice. As the original element from which all the others were created, fire is unity-in-contrariety or an emblem of God's love.

Dante's words to the speaker in "Little Gidding," comparable to Dante's own confrontations with fellow poets in the *Commedia*, occur in the modern Inferno, London in the aftermath of an air raid.* The sum of Dante's advice is to emulate the experience of Daniel, another poet:

> From wrong to wrong the exasperated spirit
> Proceeds, unless restored by that refining fire
> Where you must move in measure like a dancer.

In this condensed image are contained all suggestions developed in the whole of the *Four Quartets:* sacrifice, ritual, rebirth, and the promise of eternity. But what must not be slighted is the implication, as well, for artist and his art. Merging in the mind are Dante, Daniel, and Eliot—all poets—whose consuming preoccupation was the creation of "a pattern of timeless moments." Here the movements "in measure" affirm their power to free the poet from change, chaos, and death. Dance, at once ritual and art, individual thought and action, formalizes the purgatorial process. Arnaut's dance is a route to the Still Point and is not, the speaker protests, "an incantation/To summon the spectre of a Rose,"† a *danse macabre.* "Little Gidding" concludes with the search unending, but interestingly the moments of awareness, elusive yet precious, will be captured not only in the rose garden but "in the stillness/Between two waves of the sea," carrying us back not only to the experience of "The Dry Salvages" but to Prufrock's momentary vision of the mermaids.

In *The Family Reunion*, Eliot explores again the polar images of circling: the futile activity of the Hollow Men and the circling of the purgatorial experience. The dance that completes the play—Agatha's and Mary's circling round and round—is hinted throughout. Identifying Harry with Arnaut Daniel, Agatha (the only character who experiences an elevating vision) tells Harry:

*The experience in "Little Gidding" may be compared with W. B. Yeats's "Byzantium" in the encounter with the "blood-begotten spirits," in which the dance effects the conversion through purification from life to death: "And all complexities of fury leave. Dying into a dance. . . ."

†The ballet "Le Spectre de la Rose" often was danced by Nijinsky.

You are the consciousness of your unhappy family
Its bird sent flying through the purgatorial fire.

Most of the time, Harry knows only the wrath of the furies
and the spectre of his own anguish, translated here into the
blind circling of the damned:

> . . . many creatures moving
> Without direction, for no direction
> Leads anywhere but round and round in the vapour . . .
> In and out, in an endless drift
> Of shrieking forms in a circular desert
> Weaving with contagion of putrescent embraces
> On dissolving bone. In and out, the movement
> Until the chain broke, and I was left
> Under the single eye above the desert.

Nevertheless, Agatha's vision prevails, fulfilling her prophecy
that "when the loop in time comes—and it does not come for
everybody—/The hidden is revealed." Ultimately Harry will
be "free/From the ring of ghosts with joined hands," an image of heads stuffed with straw in their dream kingdom of
death as much as that of the avenging furies. At the close of
the play, the litany chanted by Agatha formalizes the ritual of
Purgatory, a pattern of self-denial so that "the crooked be
made straight," a recurrent motif of *Purgatorio* that reinforces
the sacramental nature of the dance:

> This way the pilgrimage
> Of expiation
> Round and round the circle
> Completing the charm. . . .

As always the Still Point is an experience realized only in
ephemeral moments in and out of time and *The Family Reunion* ends with something short of Dante's confidence in the

final canto of *Purgatorio:* "From the most holy waters I came forth, remade, even as new plants renewed with new leaves, pure and ready to mount to heaven." Instead, the plea is that

> . . . the curse be ended
> By pilgrimage
> By those who depart
> In several directions. . . .

Again, the tension that the dance images create in *The Family Reunion* is balanced between hope and despair. As late as *The Cocktail Party*, the song-and-dance tune of One-Eyed Riley shadows Celia's sacrificial experience. Eliot appended the lyric to the printed edition of the play:

> As I was walking round and round
> And round in ev'ry quarter
> I walk'd into a public house
> And order'd up my gin and water
> Too ri oo ley
> Too rii ley
> What's the matter with One-Eyed Riley.

Within the general tradition of dance imagery, we have experienced in Eliot's poetry a complex set of correlatives. Central to dance from its inception, as we know, is its significance as a beneficent ritual of imitation of god, totem, or hero in which the reenactment of a paradigmatic gesture effects a union with the divine being. As Ernst Cassirer noted: "It is no mere play that the dancer in a mythical drama is enacting; the dancer *is* the god, he *becomes* the god."[21] From its beginnings, the intrinsic qualities of the dance were not only compression, concentration, and isolation from the commonplace world but identification with a life-giving, inviolable force. Eliot once noted, "Anyone who would penetrate to the spirit of dancing . . . should begin by a close study of dancing among primitive peoples."[22] Yet when we glance at his own "primitives," the peasants of his ancestor's time in "East Coker," they lack the lustiness, the earthy quality, of Brueghel's Kermess dancers celebrated by Williams. If Eliot never associated the sexual heartiness of Williams's "satyr" with the dance, it is perhaps because *his* dance is more of a rite of transcending the flesh than a celebration of it. Crane, Roethke, and Williams all dance in their poems; for Eliot no personal experience informs his use of dance imagery. (In fact, Vivienne claimed he was a rather poor dancer!) He would never have issued Crane's winey invitation: "And you may fall downstairs with me/With perfect grace and equanimity," nor would he have portrayed himself dancing "naked, grotesquely/before my mirror/weaving my shirt round my head." Nor was he Roethke's dancing bear and waltzing prophet. Eliot would probably have viewed these postures to be more closely characteristic of apeneck Sweeney—Emerson's "Man" at the *depth* of his powers. Eliot's dance is closer, perhaps, to the Renaissance view of his distinguished forebear, Sir Thomas Elyot. In that world, the microcosmic "dauncinge, signifying matrimonie—/A dignified and commodious sacrament" reflected a larger harmony and was to be taken with due seriousness. Eliot's comment on religious dance casts some light on this view: "Is not the High Mass . . . one of the highest developments of dancing?" he asks in his essay on the ballet.[23]

Implicit in Eliot's use of the dance image are several meanings dance has accrued from its ritual beginnings. His distinct contribution, as we have seen, has been the insistent pattern of opposites. Like Siva, who reconciles destruction and creation, hope and sorrow, motion and stillness, the dance in Eliot's poetry turns on the duality of its fundamental references: as apotheosis and dance of death. The paradox is a familiar one in Eliot's symbology: desert and garden, upcoming and downgoing, time and timelessness, action and inaction. More than a dramatic device, the polarity of the images emphasizes "the horror, the horror!" in the midst of man's noblest reach for the "impossible union." In this way, the dance image, a point/counterpoint, contributes to the total design of Eliot's poetry and heightens the sense of irony we have come to associate with his vision of the world.

NOTES

1. Leonard Unger, *T. S. Eliot: Moments and Patterns* (Minneapolis: University of Minnesota Press, 1956).

2. Jung, *Man and His Symbols*, 1964, p. 25.

3. T. S. Eliot, "The Music of Poetry," in *On Poetry and Poets* (New York: Farrar, Straus, & Cudahy, 1943), p. 32.

4. See Helen L. Gardner, *The Art of T. S. Eliot* (London, 1949); Thomas R. Rees, *The Technique of T. S. Eliot* (The Hague-Paris: Mouton, 1974).

5. Bernard Bergonzi, *T. S. Eliot* (New York: Collier, 1972), pp. 74, 92.

6. Joseph Gregor, "Panorchesis," in *The Dance Has Many Faces*, ed. Sorrell, 1951, p. 136.

7. T. S. Eliot, "Ulysses, Order, and Myth," *Dial* 75, no. 5 (November 1923), p. 483.

8. T. S. Eliot, "Dante," in *Selected Essays* (New York: Harcourt, Brace & Co., 1932), p. 223.

9. Campbell, *The Hero with a Thousand Faces*, 1956, p. 128.

10. Kermode, *Romantic Image*, 1957, p. 44.

11. Frye, *Anatomy of Criticism*, 1966, p. 237.

12. David Bernstein, "The Story of Vaslav Nijinsky as a Source for T. S. Eliot's 'The Death of Saint Narcissus,' " *Hartford Studies in Literature* 4, no. 1 (Spring 1976).

13. Several variations of the ring dance appear in child lore, a few of which are offered here:

> Here we go round the mulberry bush
> The mulberry bush, the mulberry bush
> Here we go round the mulberry bush
> All on a frosty morning.
>
> Round about the rose bush
> Three steps

Follow the Dance

Four steps,
All the little boys and girls
Are sitting
On the doorsteps.

Here we go dancing jingo-ring
Jingo-ring, jingo-ring
Here we go dancing jingo-ring
About the merry-ma-tanzie.

14. Kirstein, *Dance*, 1955, p. 16.

15. Audrey T. Rodgers, "T. S. Eliot's 'Puratorio': The Structure of *Ash-Wednesday*," *Comparative LIterature Studies*, 3, no. 1 (March 1970), pp. 97–112; "The Mythic Perspective in Eliot's 'The Dry Salvages,' *Arizona Quarterly* 30, no. 1 (Spring 1974), pp. 74–94.

16. Sir Thomas Browne, *The Religio Medici and Other Writings* (London: Dent, 1960), p. 13.

17. Charles Singleton, *Dante Studies: Commedia* New York: Cambridge University Press, 1957), p. 58.

18. Drew, *T. S. Eliot*, 1949, p. 155.

19. Kermode, p. 85.

20. Raffaelo delle Columbe, quoted by Margaret Fisk Taylor, *A Time to Dance*, 1967, p. 113.

21. Ernst Cassirer, *The Philosophy of Symbolic Forms:* vol. II, *Mythical Thought*, tr. Ralph Manheim (New Haven: Yale University Press, 1955), p. 39.

22. T. S. Eliot, "The Ballet," 1967, p. 441.

23. Ibid.

CHAPTER III

The Deathless Dance: Hart Crane

And I have been given freedom and life which was acknowledged in the ecstasy of walking hand in hand across
the most beautiful bridge of the world, the cables enclosing
us and pulling us upward in such a dance as I have never
walked. . . .

In 1924, Hart Crane sent to his friend and critic, Wilbur
Underwood, a poetic fragment of *The Bridge*, explaining that
he was "on a synthesis of America and its structural identity." These "final lines" as Crane called them, never appeared in the published version of the poem:

And Midway on the structure I would stand
One moment, not as diver, but with arms
That open to project a disk's resilience
Winding the sun and planets in its face.
Water should not stem that disk, nor weigh
What holds its speed in vantage of all things
That tarnish, creep, or wane; and in like laughter,
Mobile, yet posited beyond even that time
The Pyramids shall falter, slough into sand,—
And smooth and fierce above the claim of wings,
And figured in that radiant field that rings
The Universe:—I'd have us hold one consonance
Kinetic to its poised and deathless dance.[1]

Why Crane chose finally to omit the passage remains one of those teasing literary enigmas, but clearly the lines illuminate his concern with the transfiguring vision of the poet standing on Brooklyn Bridge, arms outstretched, celebrating "that radiant field that rings/The Universe." His own artistic goal is expressed in the fusion of Poet-visionary, Bridge, and Cosmos—"one consonance." The closing dance image is central, symbolizing a harmony-in-motion intrinsic to the universe itself: timeless, graceful, immutable.

The image of the dance is crucial in Hart Crane's poetry; in this passage and elsewhere in *The Bridge* it becomes an equivalent for the kinetic energy of all living things as they "consummate their own internal rhythm";[2] but it is also an emblem of harmony and synthesis, the inviolate activity of the gods, the gestures of orgiastic celebration and the mimetic evocation of a primitive reality. Susanne Langer discusses at length this ritual of identification:

> First the actions of the "dance" would tend to become pantomimic, reminiscent of what had caused the great excitement. They would become ritualized and hold the mind to the celebrated event. . . . There would be conventional modes of dancing appropriate to certain occasions, so intimately associated with *that kind of occasion* that they would presently uphold and embody the concept of it—in other words, there would emerge symbolic gestures.[3]

In his accounts of the ritual dances of Mexico and in the Maquokeeta dance in "Powhatan's Daughter," Crane seems particularly sensitive to these nuances of meaning described by Langer.

In all of Crane's poetry, from the earliest lyrics to his longer poems, the dance externalizes a broad spectrum of experiences. For Hart Crane, as for Williams and Roethke, the dance realized his own artistic goal to "express concepts in the more direct terms of physical-psychic experience,"[4] and the challenge was to find a verbal equivalent for the art of gesture and patterned motion. To trace Crane's dance is not only to penetrate his poetic technique with greater understanding, but to inhabit, if only ephemerally, those "worlds" he perceived; "I felt the two worlds. And at once."[5] More significantly, we become a part of his own quest to *bridge* those twin realities through a network of images.

The diffusion of associations engendered by Crane's dance images testifies as much to the long history of dance itself as to the rich fabric of his imagination.

As we have seen, the themes and goals of the dance from its origins in primitive myth and ritual suffused modern dance as it developed in the early decades of the century. "Dancing is a spiritual exercise in physical form,"[6] Merce Cunningham has written; Angna Enters has emphasized the dance as a function of continuity—past with present. "Dance must crystallize a kind of similarity in human behavior down through the ages,"[7] she wrote, while Mary Wigman noted that the dance grew out of ecstasy, and "dipped into primal sources."[8] Hart Crane's dance resonates with mythic and ritualistic associations accrued in the dance over the centuries and now, as it were, reborn in the art of the modern dance that begins with Isadora.

Crane, as well as others, sought a poetic counterpart for the seemingly irreconcilable dualities of modern life. In Whitmanesque spirit—"Do I contradict myself?/Very well then I contradict myself"—Crane explored the diversities of the American experience. He chose dance images to convey his perplexed emotional states. (The *danse macabre* of Eliot's "Hollow Men," as we have seen, and Roethke's "dancing-madness" suggest this darker side.) He sought to penetrate an often hostile and unreponsive world, like Chaplin, with dance images of defiance and bravado: "We will side-step, and to the final smirk/Dally the doom of that inevitable thumb/That slowly chafes its puckered index toward us"; he tried to harmonize, where possible, the fragmented elements of experience through significant rituals, satisfying both artistically and psychologically. Like Roethke, he needed "a place to sing and dancing room."

That Crane chose dance images to convey these surging ideas and feelings reveals his renewed confidence in language that could break out of its old restraints, so that, for the first time freed from prescribed laws of esthetic perception, he, the poet, could invest it with new life. As noted in Chapter I, Joseph Frank's valuable analysis of spatialization in modern poetry reveals crucial insights into a revolutionary technique that would permit Crane and others to evolve a form of poetry for which the dance—an art defined by space and time—would be auspicious. No longer meant to perceive aspects of a poem unrolling in time, the reader of modern poetry could instead perceive elements as a collage in space, acting and interacting to produce new wholes. Pound's definition of the image as a vortex would find a vibrant and dynamic expression in Crane's poetry. So it was that the liberation of language, the emphasis on dynamism, the concept of a many-faceted image as a verbal equation of thought and emotion in constant transformation, and the attempt to utilize spatial dimensions of the poem contributed to Hart Crane's creation of dance images as a fitting metaphor for the experience of poetry. In addition, for Hart Crane, who responded excitedly all his life to the innovative developments in the world of the visual arts and the modern dance, whose structures were often imagistic collages moving in space, the choice of the dance image was natural. Here, as with all of his key metaphors, the image would carry the burden of meaning. Unlike Frost and Stevens and Eliot, Crane was not a discursive poet; the clusters of images in spatial relation in his poems communicate ideas and feelings in endless combinations. The reverberations of meaning evoked by the dance are often diverse and antithetical—much the way Eliot's own use of the dance reflects polarities. Yet there is a persistent thematic design that emerges as we examine the individual poems—motifs that we frequently associate with the poetry of transcendence.

To Hart Crane, the dance on its simplest level was the exuberant expression of an irrepressible spirit. "I am intoxicated with myself moving," Martha Graham once exclaimed, and repeatedly in Crane's poetry his celebration, a "moving all in a measure,"[9] is conveyed in a joyous, lively dance. The rhythms of the verse at times constitute a dance in themselves, so that, in Pound's terms, the *whole* poem becomes an image of dancing: the verbal equivalent for the experience. In Crane's poetry, reminiscent of Yeats's, the dance attempts to harmonize the duality in the mind of the poet for whom antithesis is the very nature of existence, seeking in the dance a means whereby the natural and supernatural conjoin: "Marbles of the dancing floor/Break bitter furies of complexity," in the Byzantium of the imagination. Aware that the activity of *spanning* the void between two realities may be the only means of reconciling them, Crane often chooses images of bridges, rivers, seas, and trains; but as frequently, his dances are a *process* of whirling toward universal harmony whether in the vortex of the sea as he invokes it to "bind us in time" or in the brief contact of human and divine, as in "The Bridge of Estador":

> O Beauty's fool, though you have never
> Seen them again, you won't forget,
> Nor the Gods that danced before you
> When your fingers spread among stars.

The yearning to fuse, harmonize, transcend the opposites in his disparate worlds often produced a dance ritual that is numinous, if ephemeral. If a *lasting* unity and perfection in a world of polarities, change, and chaos were elusive and impermanent, at least Crane's visionary gift to "see thro' the eye," as Blake affirmed, permitted brief glimpses of the "unfractured idiom" other poets had experienced: Roethke's "vision of the world as dancing people," Williams's "dance in measure"—gleaming intimations in a search for the coherent

63

world they sensed within. With his eye on *Paradiso*, Eliot could still admit, "this is the aim/Never here to be realised;/Who are only undefeated/Because we have gone on trying." The struggle to sustain his vision may be traced in Crane's images of the dance.

Hart Crane's was a visual imagination. Like all mythic poets from Dante's time until his own, Crane believed in the harmonizing vision of the poet that seeks to proclaim and celebrate the universal Oneness. As we have seen, the triumph of the mythic vision is the victory over time, the apotheosis whereby man transcends change and disorder—the leap into eternity. And only in myth, Genesius Jones writes, "does the poet find an organ of consciousness which embodies the alogical, the alchemic, the magical, and the cosmogonous in sensual form."[10] Crane sought to create an American myth, accented, like all myths, with spiritual luminousness. He wrote in 1923, "The modern artist needs gigantic assimilative capacities, emotion,—and the greatest of all—vision. I feel myself quite fit to become a suitable *Pindar* for the dawn of the machine age."[11] His own mythic view—so much a part of the Whitman tradition—with its perception of the poet as prophet: "He is the arbiter of the diverse. . . . He is the seer," would be compatible with the visionary, if romantic, quest of modern dance. Hart Crane found in myth's transcendent objective and ritual's reassuring design a means for expressing a new ideal. He would follow Whitman, who, he professed, "was able to coordinate those forces in America which seem most intractable, fusing them into a universal vision which takes on additional significance as time goes on."[12] What Crane affirmed as well was the energizing quality that informs objects that traditionally carried mythic overtones: the river, the sea, the earth as Pocahontas. Manifestations of elemental motion, they are always associated with a life-giving mystique. As we shall see in *The Bridge*, their "activity" is often expressed as a dance. And only the poet-seer, "in touch" with the process and the power, could convey the ineffable mysteries to other men. To Gorham Munson he wrote in 1922, recounting what today we would call a "trip" into that special world induced by drugs:

> At times, . . . I feel an enormous power in me—that seems almost supernatural. If this power is not too dissipated in aggravations and discouragements, I may amount to something sometime. I can say this with perfect equanimity because I am notoriously drunk and the victrola is still going with that glorious Bolero. Did I tell you of that thrilling experience this last winter in the dentist's chair when under the influence of ether and *amnesia* my mind spiralled to a kind of seventh heaven of consciousness and egoistic dance among the seven spheres—and something like an objective voice kept saying to me—"You have the higher consciousness—you have the higher consciousness." . . . I felt the two worlds. And at once.

The experience, it is true, was too often ephemeral. Too frequently, beset by personal problems and self-doubt, he would write, "It is hard to dance in proper measure," but his search for the harmonizing vision and his Platonic confidence in that "other reality" sustained him through much of his poetic career. For all Crane's "idealism" his dance was often Dionysian—an association he found compatible with his own view of the nature of man and the artist. The complex and contrasting patterns evoked by the god comprise the mosaic of Crane's life and art as well: joyous and tragic, orgiastic and transcendent, creative and destructive. As Crane expressed his wine-inspired poetic function:

> . . . Wine talons
> Build freedom up about me and distill
> This competence. . . .

In many ways, Crane's personal life, so indisputably linked to his poetry, expressed the tragedy implicit in the myth of

Dionysus. He alternated between frenzied exultation and deep despair; he pursued both his creative quest and his self-destruction with equal zest. To his friends he was a "roaring boy," the "voyager," the modern Whitman celebrating himself, the disarming and impossible genius, and always the dancer. Dancing was Crane's chief personal mode of expression. From his early childhood, it served the cathartic function of releasing his inner frustrations, exorcizing his devils. Often with the help of wine, he would spin himself into orgies of motion that, on occasion, achieved moments of real grace and beauty. Charmion von Wiegand recalls such a moment:

> Suddenly there was a space in the middle of the room, and there was Hart dancing with abandon by himself. And he really had such rhythm. I knew he was tight, but it was very beautiful. Because he had absolute abandon and, at the same time, a certain control of his movements, he was like a ballet dancer swinging there—and he was having a gorgeous time.[13]

At times, she tells us, "Hart's dancing, frantic and desperate, ended in collapse." Another friend, Nathan Asch, writes of the orgiastic dancing at Crane's parties reminiscent of "some primeval horde," after which "everything collapsed." One of the most sensitive recollections comes from Isadore Schneider, who saw in Crane the consummate figure of the artist in whom both dancing and poetry united:

> I thought of him as the most complete artist that I had ever met. By that I mean that I felt that he was an artist to his fingertips, that he was an artist in almost every respect of even daily living. He was not only interested in literature, he was interested in all the arts; and his interest was always an intimate and intense one. . . . He walked as if he were dancing. There was a grace in his movements. They were those of a dancer. . . . I always felt, "I am in the presence of an artist."

That Crane thought of himself as a dancer is a recurrent theme in his letters, especially when he attempted to communicate the intensity of his feelings of love. The rhythm of movement in nature, the "dance of the river" is one that, we shall see, is the life-giving activity in "Powhatan's Daughter"; it gives back to the poet-lover an image of his own completeness. Crane thought a good deal about the artists who were dancers and frequently identified himself with them. One of his poems is dedicated to his close friend, Stanislaw Portapovitch, a dancer with Diaghilev's Ballet Russe, who taught him many things, notably the *gozotsky*, which he demonstrated on every occasion. To Carl Schmitt, the dancer exerted a distinct influence on Crane: "Portapovitch demonstrated both in conversation and in art the crucial importance of balance. It was inevitably after his visits with Portapovitch that Crane would be most filled with an ebullient sense of life's possibilities." Crane was deeply moved by Isadora Duncan as well, and after seeing her perform in Cleveland in 1922, he wrote to Munson:

> It was glorious beyond words, and sad beyond words, too, from the rude and careless reception she got here. It was like a wave of life, a flaming gale that passed over the heads of the nine thousand in the audience . . . with such intensity of gesture and such plastique grace as I have never seen. . . . I felt like rushing to the stage.

But perhaps the most revealing personal account comes from Crane himself when he experienced the ritual tribal dances in Mexico only weeks before his death. He had come, he wrote his stepmother, Bess Crane, to the feast of the Virgin of Guadaloupe in Mexico City to see some native Indian dances:

> The whole business is simply indescribable . . . suffice it to say that the dances were wonderful. . . . The dancing is all very serious and very set and formal; it generally derives

67

from very ancient tribal rites. . . . The figure of the Virgin of Guadaloupe miraculously unites the teachings of the early Catholic missionaries with many survivals of the old Indian myths and pagan cults. She is a typically Mexican product, a strange blend of Christian and pagan strains. What a country and a people!

Only days later, at the feast of Tepoztecatl, the elders invited him to share their ritual celebration, putting in his hands the drumsticks to beat out the rhythm:

> It seemed too good to be true, really, that I . . . should be invited to actually participate. And actually I did! I not only beat the exact rhythm with all due accents, which they had been keeping up for hours; I even worked in an elaboration, based on the lighter tattoo of the more modern drum. . . . I had the pleasure of pleasing them so that they almost embraced me. They did, in fact, several of them— put their arms around our shoulders and walk back and forth the whole length of the roof, when at the astronomical hour of six the whole place seemed to go mad in the refulgence of full day. . . . You can't imagine how exciting it was to be actually a part of their ritual.

What the dance of the elders accomplished, as he tells us, was the spiritual fusion of two antithetical faiths, "two voices, still in conflict in Mexico, the idol's and the Cross'," becoming in the dance miraculously one. Thus had the experience of Tepoztecatl fulfilled the visionary dream in "The Dance," where, united with the Indian Maquokeeta, the poet danced himself "back the tribal morn."

All his life Hart Crane danced. It is no accident, therefore, that the activity would be transformed into a crucial image in his poetry. Crane's earliest lyrics reveal the images and poetic technique that would constitute his idiom in the maturer poems. His experimentation reflected, as we have noted, his enthusiasm for the Imagists as well as the Symbolist poetry of LaForgue, Mallarmé, and Rimbaud. Like Rimbaud's "Bateau Ivre," Baudelaire's image of the dancing soul, "And my soul danced, danced like an old lighter/Without masts, on a monstrous shoreless sea," became for poets like Crane their own emblem for the condition of man in the modern world. LaForgue echoes this motif at the end of his "Complaint of That Good Moon":

> Under the empty
> Canopy
> We are dancing, we are dancing
> Under the empty
> Canopy
> Swiftly dancing in a ring

LaForgue's theme of a *danse macabre*, developed later by Eliot in his circling hollow men, would have been familiar to Crane, who used the image in "The Wine Menagerie." His mode of splicing images is reminiscent of the early Eliot poems; both poets fuse designs of image clusters to evoke a single mood. The parallels between the two poet-apprentices extend beyond the impact of Pound's Imagist Movement to Eliot's own preoccupation with LaForgue, Corbière, and other Symbolists and his own consistent habit of raiding his earlier poetry for useful symbols, notably the dance which figures largely in his poetry and which first appeared in "The Death of St. Narcissus."

In Crane's case, "The Moth That God Made Blind," written at the age of seventeen, deals for the first time with poetic vision. The patterned movements of the blind moth as it mounts upward toward the dazzling sun suggest the motions of dance. As he climbs toward his moment of illumination, he is described as "pierroting over,—/Swinging in spirals round the fresh breasts of day," the image of a blind Pierrot fusing with the tragic absurdity of the rollicking clown. In a moment when he is "still gyrating," he experiences the transfiguring vision, the sun giving back a cosmic dance of its own in the rays "seething and rounding in long streams of light." For the poet, as for the moth, the vision is ephemeral, but he too has "hugged beauty and winged life's brief spell." Since only dance partakes of both time and space, the unifying activity, however transient, is rewarding. The search to recapture the fleeting vision in the moth's arching pattern will bring the poet to *The Bridge*, where, more successfully, the seagull's wings that "dip and pivot him" will initiate his own upward journey. Thus from the first, the dance in Crane's symbology will be identified both with vision, unity, and aspiration and with the impairment of vision and death as well. Here the blind moth, permitted a brief moment of perception in which the unity of all things is recognized, plunges instantly to earth and destruction. The slight poem, while not poetically convincing, is nonetheless interesting as an experiment.

In "October-November," the entire action of this imagist exercise—and it is a little more—is a movement in space. The verbs suggest strong physical motions as the sun "whips away the mists, Dives through the filter of trellises." Its colours "scintillate/On trees that seem dancing/in delirium," calling up a Dionysian revelry in nature. A similar spirit infuses "Carmen de Boheme," in which Carmen's sinuous dance creates at once a vision of sensuality and transcendence. The triple associations of wine, dance, and vision which will figure again in "The Wine Menagerie," and become developed more successfully in "For the Marriage of Faustus and Helen," are presented here in the "absinthe-drinking women," in Carmen's wild swirling motions: "Akimbo arms and smouldering eyes; . . . Carmen whirls, and music swirls and dips," and in the beauty of the recollected moment: "And some dream still of Carmen's mystic face,—/Yellow, Pallid, like ancient lace." For Crane, dancing was frequently cathartic, as we have seen in the personal recollections. In his short poem to Portapovitch, the activity of release culminates in art that is "more real than life." For Portapovitch's dance lingers in the corridors of memory, "haunting the blank stage with lingering alarms." The strong opening verb accents the efficacy of action, the "leap" that is simultaneously aspiration and self-fulfillment for the hero-clown. The reference to Daphnis evokes not only the pastoral romance that inspired Ravel's "Daphnis and Chloe," commissioned by Diaghilev for his Ballet Russe in 1912 and danced by Portapovitch, but suggests as well the mythical son of Hermes who, in the heightened sensitivity induced by wine, produced songs that ushered in pastoral music. Crane's loving tribute to his friend is an affirmation of the permanence of art long after the dance is over. Merging in the consciousness are not only Portapovitch the dancer, but clown, poet, singer, and hero—consummate artists all.

By the time Crane wrote "The Bridge of Estador," the dance had already assumed new depths of meaning for him beyond the sensual activity expressing joy or despair or sexual exuberance. As we have seen in "To Portapovitch," the mere lingering feelings of pleasure or release intensify into mystical communions. "The Bridge of Estador" for the first time presents Crane's central symbol for unifying his two worlds: a bridge that spans his world of the ideal and modern technological America. The poem begins with the exhortation to "walk high on the bridge of Estador," where ultimately the undivided, harmonious cosmos will be revealed. For the first time, Crane invests the dance with the activity of the gods. Later, Crane will envision the dance as the apotheosis of *The Bridge* and will celebrate the dance of the seas in the haunting *Voyages II*. Here in "The Bridge of Estador" the achieved vision, though ephemeral, is unforgettable. The knowledge the moment yields, even for those who "are twisted with the love/Of things irreconcilable," will be etched in the memory. As Crane tells them: "though you have never/Seen them again, you won't forget." The testimony of the dancing gods defies the world of antitheses and affirms reconciliation among the stars. It is this conviction that leads the poet to urge his fellow poets to "follow your arches/To what corners of the sky they pull you to,—" in the hope of redeeming the transitory vision. As Pierrot, the sensitive capering clown, or Gargantua, the bawdy Rabelaisian comic, the poet can, as he tells us in the beginning, walk "where no one has ever walked there before." The poem is most interesting as a stage in the development of Crane's greater achievements in *The Bridge*.

Even in the darkness of the wasteland city, the poet achieves a pleasurable moment. In "Porphyro in Akron," the poet Porphyro, finding himself in the alien, culturally arid city, identifies with the Sunday fiddlers who play "ragtime and dance before the door," when later in his rooms the moment haunts him, feeling his "toes/Are ridiculously tapping/The spindles at the foot of the bed." The rhythm of the dance effects the union, momentary but pleasant, of poet and artist.

"The Wine Menagerie" strikes the same scene but juxtaposes the image of dance as art in Stravinsky's "Petrouchka" with a *danse macabre* of the modern city. The backdrop is a sleazy cocktail lounge—the wine menagerie where the "animals" commingle; the air is one of depravity, comedy, grotesquery as images of the decapitated Holofernes and John the Baptist float up with the dancing zombies, "poor streaked bodies wreathing up and out." Amid the ugliness and human squalor, the poet, his sight improved rather than impaired by his half-drunken state, experiences a heightened awareness. Reaching beyond the tawdry group, he senses within himself

> New thresholds, new anatomies! Wine talons
> Build freedom up about me and distill
> This competence—to travel in a tear
> Sparkling alone, within another's will
>
> Until my blood dream a receptive smile
> Wherein new purities are shared . . .

The distillation, born first of winey compassion and then of hell and anguish, enables him to see beauty: "Between black tusks the roses shine." Moreover, he becomes the poet of their sordid souls, like the Pierrot who also travels in a tear, "sparkling alone, within another's will." The oblique parallels with Fokine's adaptation of "Petrouchka" are crucial. We recall the ballet set in a carnival atmosphere, the drunken men milling around, the organ grinder playing as the showman, the Charlatan, begins his puppet show. The drama presents Petrouchka, the sensitive and suffering poet-lover, the Ballerina, the "valentine" who refuses him and breaks his heart, and the Moor, epitome of brute force and stupidity, who kills him. At the end of the ballet, Petrouchka's ghost dances back to haunt the Charlatan who has not foreseen that his creation would achieve a soul. Crane's image thus conjures up a network of associations: the ballet itself, the poet-singer-puppet who assumes a soul through suffering, and the Ballerina pivoting on her pin as miraculously as the countless angels. The poet of "The Wine Menagerie," merging with the soul of Petrouchka, walks away to fold *his* exile on his back again, dancing his suffering and theirs into poetry. This is the accomplishment of his redeeming sight "wherein new purities are snared." Clearly Crane is experimenting in the poem with the Dionysian implications of tragedy: the vision, quickened by the wine, of death and rebirth and immortality through suffering to art.

Crane's hope that the artist could defeat the world lay at the base of his lifelong admiration for Charlie Chaplin. Only months before his death, he sought out a Chaplin rerun in a shabby theater in Mexico City. Peggy Cowley described their experience: "Tears streamed down our faces and we clung to each other laughing louder than anyone else in the house. The greatest mime of the century had brought the orchids and the rags together in joint appreciation." Years earlier, when Crane wrote "Chaplinesque," he explained the poem as "a sympathetic attempt to put into words some of

Charlie's pantomime, so beautiful, and so full of eloquence."
The figure of Crane's clown-tramp owes much to a whole
tradition of archetypal clowns but fundamentally Crane's
model was the early Chaplin of *City Lights*. Chaplin's comedy was all gesture, what today one calls "body language";
each movement was a poke at a whole hostile universe and a
triumph of his self-survival. In every facial expression or turn
of his body, Chaplin laid bare the essential absurdity of life, a
role Crane had envisioned for his own in "The Bridge of
Estador," seen through "the everlasting eyes of Pierrot/Or, of
Gargantua, the laughter." From the opening lines, the poet
identifies himself with Charlie's art: "We make our meek
adjustments." The poem has a spatial dimension in which
Charlie's dance—if we so call it—isolates him from the commonplace and merges him with a life-giving, inviolable force.
Charlie is figured in the "slithered pockets," the innocence
and surprise, but most of all he emerges in the memorable
sidesteps, collapses, and in the pirouetting cane recalling his
own balletic gestures. Evasion becomes first covert rebellion
and then transcendence even as the empty ashcan is transformed into a grail of laughter. The capering Charlie evokes
all humanity as the kitten in the wilderness, Eliot's "notion of
some infinitely gentle/Infinitely suffering thing." As Charlie's
dance harmonizes poet and clown, artist and fool, so the
poem itself bridges the gap between language and gesture,
becoming the verbal equivalent of Charlie's act. "Chaplinesque" thus becomes another image in Crane's idiom of symbolic motion. It remains one of Crane's most compressed and
intensely moving portraits of the artist as clown as well as a
superb translation of Charlie's dance into language.

"For the Marriage of Faustus and Helen" presents again
the now familiar motif of wine, dance, and vision. Clearly,
Crane's ideas of a Dionysian creator-destroyer had coalesced
into an important symbol in his poetry. Dionysus evokes a
host of multiple echoes: the dying and reviving god whose
suffering and pain led to insight and immortality; the de-

monic and irrational force in man's soul; the joyful, exuberant
deity of wine and fertility. Thus the theme of transcendence
through ecstasy, which we have experienced elsewhere in
Crane's poetry, illuminates "Faustus and Helen."

Despite the fine explications of "For the Marriage of Faustus and Helen," the most helpful clues come from Crane
himself, who discussed the poem frequently in his letters and
in "General Aims and Theories":

> So I found "Helen" sitting in a street car; the Dionysian
> revels of her court and her seduction were transferred to a
> Metropolitan roof garden with a jazz orchestra; and the
> *katharsis* of the fall of Troy I saw approximated in the
> recent World War. The importance of this scaffolding may
> easily be exaggerated, but it gave me a series of correspon-
> dences between two widely separated worlds on which to
> sound some major themes of human speculation—love,
> beauty, death, renascence.[14]

Here, in a poem of sustained length, Crane "felt the two
worlds. And at once," and the means through which he links
them becomes the action of the poem. The archetypal search
of the poet, Faust, for a union with eternal beauty, Helen,
leads to communion with the "eternal gunman"—the "spirit
of Dionysian surrender," as Alan Trachtenberg observes.[15]
The creative spirit emerges in the orgiastic intoxication with
modern jazz and dance, as the union with the sensual Helen
precedes the moment when the poet Faustus will "praise the
years," when his "imagination spans beyond despair." Like
Dionysus, the "wine-inspired prophet" achieves a single vision which redeems his world and makes it possible for art.

The dance in "Faustus and Helen" is one of several images
of spanning motion Crane will use in a poem that already
focuses on the building of "bridges." Its function is revealed
indirectly in Crane's own criticism of the pessimism of modern
poets reflected in their "Dance of Death." Crane turns *his*

dance into a Dance of Life that validates "the world dimensional for those untwisted by the love of things irreconcilable."

A first glance at "Faustus and Helen I" unfolds the world of "appearances," a divided, "stock-exchange" world that nonetheless is "brushed by sparrow wings" and hints of promise "somewhere/Virginal perhaps, less fragmentary, cool." From this point, the tempo is stepped up, as the voyaging poet embarks on his search for "a world dimensional." The images suggest gesture and motion: the poet on the moving streetcar, "lost yet poised in traffic," reaches out to touch the smiling Helen whose hands "count the nights." The gliding earth and the gliding car merge as he invokes ideal beauty: "But if I lift my arms it is to bend/To you who turned away once, Helen." Finally, as his vision encloses the ideal city, he praises Helen, amid the beating life of the real city's "companion ways." This sense of the pulsing rhythm of the city is a prelude to the jazzing dancers of Part II. The intrusion of the city is not incompatible with the figure of Helen in whom Lewis sees a kind of "carnal frivolity" suggesting both her ideal and erotic qualities, corresponding to "the inseparable and contradictory desires of man."[16] It is these dual aspects of love that the dance will harmonize ultimately in *The Bridge*, but here in Part I we prepare for the orgiastic dancing of "The Siren of the Springs of Guilty Song," Crane's first title for "Faustus and Helen II."

The poem opens on the jazz world of Harlem and the madly whirling dancers of the roof garden. Crane knew well the importance of dance to jazz music. As Jean D'Udine reminds us in *L'Art et le Geste*, "All music is a dancing. . . . All melody is a series of attitudes."[17] Crane's own sense of identity with musicians is reinforced by D'Udine's observation that "every artist is a transformer; all artistic creation is but a transmutation." Jazz music and its accompanying dance were expressive of a soaring, liberating spirit among the black artists of the twenties as well as their own tough response to the facts of despair, hardship, and pessimism.

Crane appreciated the fundamental tension intrinsic in black music: spontaneous, artistic, individualized, yet at the same time cathartic and transcendent. It is this spirit he attempted to translate into verbal equivalents in "Faustus and Helen II." The intensity of the musicians and the dancers culminates in a wild self-abandonment:

> Brazen hypnotics glitter here;
> Glee shifts from foot to foot,
> Magnetic to their tremolo.
>
> This crashing opera bouffe,
> Blest excursion! this ricochet
> From roof to roof—

As Herbert Leibowitz notes, "Everything jumps and steps."[18]* The music of the jazzers is gay, orgiastic; the dancers complement the musical rhythms: "White shadows slip across the floor/Splayed like cards from a loose hand." The images evoke dualities: on the one hand suggesting a tribal ritual, daemonic and mysterious, while on the other recalling the erotic abandon of Crane's own drunken orgies, at once cathartic and artistic: "And you may fall downstairs with me/With perfect grace and equanimity."† In this world of guilty laughter and dance, "gyrating awnings," and the "divine grotesque," Faust discovers, "this music has a reassuring way." The last stanza is the dance, of Faustus pursuing Helen as they move "among slim skaters of the gardened skies." The "incandescent wax" may well be the modern dance floor or, as Lewis suggests, the phonograph record

---

*Lewis comments upon the passage: "It [This crashing opera bouffe] was the way human life itself felt to Crane at this time: a dance, and not a Dance of Death, but a dance of joyful life."[19]

†Leibowitz notes: "The pattern of the dance leads to unexpected changes, from ellipse to a loping, bouncing gait, and so does the language.... The poet is both cool spectator and participant in the dance.... This is in part a 'blest excursion.' "[20]

turning out the siren's song "for human life to dance to; it will lighten and alleviate the shadings of anxieties, the frailties we inherit as human beings."[21] Either interpretation serves Crane's meaning here since most of Crane's dancing was done to accompaniment of an endless number of dance records he carried around with him! More critical here is the transformation of the earlier wild revelry into "perfect grace" and art, as the poet-spectator becomes the dancer.[22]

The last part of the poem completes the "experience" of Faustus in merging not only with Helen but with other men in a "mysterious Primordial unity," as Dembo suggests.[23] Crane had explained "Faustus and Helen III" as "Dionysian in its attitude, the creator and the eternal destroyer dance arm in arm."[24] Thus perception "begins in suffering and surrender to pain for insight it brings."[25] The poem is tragic in tone, as the poet Faustus invokes us: "Let us unbind our throats of fear and pity." The religious gunman is the creator-destroyer who alone determines beauty in the street and who finally will lead Faustus to remember, to survive, to "persist to speak again," and, last, to "delve upward." The experience is an archetype of death and rebirth. In the final lines, the poet defeats death and time, becoming the bridge himself to the other world: "Delve upward for the new and scattered wine,/O brother-thief of time, that we recall." The idiom is still Dionysian but Helen is now the transcendent ideal toward which he has traveled. The final image of the poem is a stunning incarnation of the tragic world as dancer. The years are, as Lewis suggests, the "world bloodied by war and condemned by man,"[26] but it seems that more is at work here. The gestures of a suffering world whose "bleeding hands extend and thresh the height," evoke the dancers Crane knew when he was composing the poem: the jazz dancers, the abused Isadora, and Hart himself. The poet's hymn of praise encloses them all, his own imagination spanning their despair. The dance image closes the poem: the "gestures" of the suffering years are complemented by the motion of the imagination, "out-pacing bargain, vocable, and prayer." The concept of the bridging poetic imagination has been, as we have seen, the *action* of the entire three poems that link his "two widely separated worlds," and so necessary to a poet who wrote at this time: "We who create must endure—must hold to spirit not by the mind, by intellect alone. . . . I find my imagination more sufficient all the time."[27] That the imagination could hold in perfect harmony all the disparate elements of the American experience would be the underlying conviction for his mythic poem, *The Bridge*. As early as "My Grandmother's Love Letters," Crane expressed the need to *span* his two worlds—here, the past and present, but later, often the simultaneous worlds of real and ideal, "Over the greatness of such space/Steps must be gentle./It is all hung with an invisible white hair." He was always to associate divinity with an integrative function: his God would be a bridge. The theme is germinal in "The Bridge of Estador," and more fully explored in "For the Marriage of Faustus and Helen," until it assumes major symbolic significance in *The Bridge*. As seen earlier, the creative activity of a god is often expressed in Crane's poetry in terms of rhythmic motion: an arching, vaulting, leaping, dancing spirit that reconciles opposites. In his role as poet-visionary, he often conceived of himself as a human bridge, so that like Yeats's golden bird, the artist merges with his art. The idea is expressed frequently in modern poetry, by Yeats, "O body swayed to music, O brightening glance,/How can we know the dancer from the dance?" or by Eliot: "You are the music/While the music lasts."

That *The Bridge* does not finally sustain that mythic vision scarcely minimizes the grandeur of the undertaking, the integrity of the fleeting epiphanies, the brilliance of the images. The design of the poem is one of time and space, culminating in the defeat of both; *The Bridge*, despite its spiritual lows, ends on this triumph:

So to thine Everpresence, beyond time,
Like spears ensanguined of one tolling star
That bleeds infinity—the orphic strings,
Sidereal phalanxes, leap and converge:
One Song, One Bridge of Fire!

The choice of a symbol from the technological world, Brooklyn Bridge, the motif of a "mystical synthesis," and the tempo of music and dance figured on Crane's drawing board from the poem's inception. Elatedly he wrote Munson, "Such a waving of banners, such ascents of towers, such dancing, etc., will never have been put down on paper. The form will be symphonic."[28] Even as late as 1927, he explained the poem in musical terms: the "Ave Maria" was a "sea-swell crescendo"; "The Harbor Dawn," a legato; he spoke of the "quickening rhythms" of "Van Winkle," and the "strident tempo" of jazz in "The River." As for "The Dance," he noted cryptically, "it was just that—a dance." It is clear that for Crane, as for other Imagist poets, the whole poem could constitute a single image. Such poems as Williams's *Paterson* and Pound's *Cantos* support the innovative structuring of images Crane suggested above.

The great spanning bridge would be transmuted into other "bridges"; Columbus's ship linking the continents, the westward-moving train uniting Far Rockaway with Golden Gate, the mythic Mississippi joining East, West, North, and South; the dance of Pocahontas and Maquokeeta, a primitive rite bringing man to God. The efficacy of physical action is of course central to all myth. We recall in the Bhagavad Gita the advice Arjuna receives from the disguised god, Krishna, that only through action can man achieve apotheosis. Here in *The Bridge*, in a symbolic voyage westward in space and backward in time, the poet could, he tells us, "handle the beautiful skeins of this myth of America," in which "the initial impulses of 'our people' " will be "gathered up toward the climax of the bridge, symbol of our constructive future, our unique identity."

In "Proem," prayer, prophecy, and poetic prologue, Crane announces this aspiration. At first we experience the divergent worlds: the sacred realm of the gull as it dips, pivots, and arches in perfect rings over the bay, its motions testifying to its purity, inviolability, and beauty in nature; and the profane world: suicidal, fragmented, and tragic. The spirit the poet invokes is the harmonizing Presence across the harbor, whose power not only effects the divine reconciliation of opposites, but who grants the poet himself the ineffable vision of wholeness: "Unto us lowliest sometime sweep, descend/ And of the curveship lend a myth to God." Thus the bridge affirms his own integrative powers that will make possible the creation of a new myth, a new representation of spiritual reality in a broken world. All the images describe the bridge's divine nature. The bridge is all motion yet stillness, freedom yet restraint, manmade yet Primum Mobile. Its lights are beads on a rosary yet it is "unfractured idiom." The bridge is the mother, the graceful Pietà lifting night in her arms, but the movements also suggest the balletic gestures of a powerful dancer. He vaults, sweeps, descends, his motions imitating the curving arcs of the gull. Thus Bridge-God-Dancer reconciles sacred and profane, fuses the "prayer of parish, and the lover's cry." The poet perceives that "all is One," as Lucretius observed, and his vision, like Dante's own, stretches to the stars.[29]

The sections of *The Bridge* that follow the "Proem" reinforce the structure of movement in time and space. It is not possible to detail here all the images of motion that precede Maquokeeta's dance, but even an overview reveals the tension created between hope and despair, life and death that shapes the voyage. In "Ave Maria," as Columbus's ship speeds homeward on treacherous waters, the images suggest both a dance of death and a dance of life. The sea's cresting, creeping, troughing activity is both seductive and ominous as the waves "climb the dusk," their "green crying towers a-sway." Elsewhere in "Voyages I," Crane had explored the attraction and danger of the sea, where "the sun beats lightning on the waves,/The waves fold thunder on the sand." He warns the innocent children on the beach: "The bottom of the sea is cruel." Again, in "Voyages II," the seas are gay "adagios of islands," but almost instantly he senses the vortex that pulls us toward the grave.

In "Ave Maria," the movements of the cosmos itself are celebrated in "this turning rondure whole," and the "one sapphire wheel," which reflect God in their circles of infinity: "The Orbic wake of thy once whirling feet,/Elohim, still I hear they sounding heel!" Crane's image of a dancing god is traditional: medieval accounts of a dancing Jesus are abundant, just as dances were for much of man's history an expression of his spiritual union with God.

"Powhatan's Daughter" introduces Pocahontas, primitive body of America with whom he, the poet, seeks to unite. We meet her first dancing naked in the marketplace with the rowdy boys, her youth and exuberance suggesting a wild, irrepressible gaiety and innocence. She is the siren who will enter the poet's morning dream and "stealthily weave us into day," whose "cool arms murmurously about me lay." Pocahontas becomes the American Circe: her beauty, sensuality, and freedom revealed in her graceful gestures. In the dream of "The Harbor Dawn," she hints of the consummation to come: "Who is the woman with us at dawn . . . who is the flesh our feet have moved upon?" the confused dreamer asks. His answer comes in "The River," but not until he moves backward in time to travel the route of American history. The images of motion are of the train that traverses "the body of America"; the music is that of the hurdy-gurdy as the train dances speedily on its way. On the Twentieth Century Limited, we are hurtled through space: the train whistles, hurries, whizzes, merges with running brooks, straddles the hills, "a dance of wheel on wheel." The dance becomes the agent of transfiguration as the modern train merges with the flowing Mississippi. Again Crane sounds the dance of death as the Mississippi casts up memories of the American tragedy; we drift in stillness, sliding prone, lost in the tideless spell as we hear "a liquid theme that floating niggers swell." The jazz rhythms of conflicting lament and aspiration form the river god's dance as it meets the sea. The movements, fast and slow, hopeful and despairing, symbolize the deeper reality of the American experience. And Pocahontas, mythical America, subdues both time and space. The poet learns to know her as he travels her length and depth:

> . . . But I knew her body there,
> Time like a serpent down her shoulder, dark,
> And space, an eaglet's wing, laid on her hair.

The beauty and sensuality of the Indian girl and the poet's subjugation of her evoke all the implications of the dance as an act of sexual consummation. The morning vision will prefigure the union of Pocahontas and Maquokeeta, the Indian brave, and finally of the poet-visionary and America itself.

In a letter to Otto Kahn, Crane detailed the newly created section, "The Dance": "Here one is on the pure mythical and smoky soil at last! Not only do I describe the conflict between the two races in this dance—I also become identified with the Indian and his world before it is over." The theme of "The Dance" was to be a pattern of the death and rebirth of the Indian brave Maquokeeta as he becomes united at last with nature in the image of Pocahontas. The importance of this section to the structure of the whole poem cannot be overstressed. Lewis noted, "It is the very heart and center of the epic movement, . . . Crane's ultimate dance: the fulfillment not only of the circling dance of God Columbus had perceived in the planetary wheel, but also . . . the fulfillment of all dances that had animated Crane's poetry from 'The Bridge of Estador.' "[30]

The ritual dance of Pocahontas, Maquokeeta, and finally
the poet himself has its source in tribal dances of primitive
societies. Mircea Eliade has described the rite that com-
memorates the sacred moment of beginnings, thus, in a symbolic rebirth, returning man to god. The ritual celebrates the
unity of the cosmos, the transfiguration of man—here in the
doomed American Indian—and the mystical reconciliation of
opposites. Crane wrote: "Pocahontas (the continent) survives
the extinction of the Indian, who finally after being assumed
into the elements of nature . . . persists only as a kind of 'eye'
in the sky, or as a star that hangs between day and night."[31]
Thus we witness three transformations in the poem: the rebirth of the Earth Goddess through union with her lover, the
Indian rain dancer; the metamorphosis of Maquokeeta, the
brave, as a star in the heavens according to Indian myth; and
finally the transfiguration of the poet who becomes the tribal
medicine man, not merely witnessing the divine union but
becoming participant—dancing with Maquokeeta, taming
the serpent of time and the eagle of space, invoking his own
creative power to "dance us back the tribal morn!"

The poem opens with the vision of death and rebirth in the
seasons of the year. The entire action is a ballet as the earth
goddess, squired by her lover, reveals herself first as the
"glacier woman": "She ran the neighing canyons all the
spring!/She spouted arms; she rose with maize—to die." The
whole vision is informed by the sensuality, divinity, and
breathless beauty of Pocahontas as she awaits her fulfillment
in her lover, his death to become her life. The poet sees with
the eyes of the Indian brave, Maquokeeta: "I could see/Your
hair's crescent running, and the blue/First moth of evening
take wing stealthily." He accelerates upward toward a better
vision of her, his swift, light movements those of an Indian
himself as he crosses through the waters, rises to the mountain pass, speeding over bluffs, tarns, and streams—his own
motions a correlative for his "blood remembering its first
invasion of her secrecy." The images are sexual in nature,

anticipating the dance of nature that follows: Pocahontas's yearning for her lover. The threshing, swooping, kneeling, circling, crashing activity in nature mirrors back her own frustrated desire. "The long moan of a dance is in the sky," the poet observes, then commands the Indian brave: "Dance Maquokeeta: Pocahontas grieves." The stanzas that follow become the verbal equivalent of Maquokeeta's dance of agony as, in the earlier lines, the poet's rhythms revealed the soul of Pocahontas's imagined being. Sacrificed at the stake, the Indian becomes the risen god; so the poet invokes the brave to dance out his destiny:

> Dance, Maquokeeta! snake that lives before
> That casts his pelt, and lives beyond! Sprout, horn!
> Spark, tooth! Medicine-man, relent, restore—
> Lie to us,—dance us back the tribal morn!

Simultaneously, the poet merges with the dancing Maquokeeta:

> ... I, too, was liege
> To rainbows currying each pulsant bone:
> Surpassed the circumstance, danced out the siege!

As the Indian is absorbed into the cosmos, the life in the sky of Indian myth, the speaker testifies to the miracle of transcendence: "I saw thy change begun." The images, which recall the qualities of the gull and the great bridge of "Proem," carry connotations of divine union:

> And saw thee dive to kiss that destiny
> Like one white meteor, sacrosanct and blent
> At last with all that's consummate and free
> There, where the first and last gods keep thy tent.

The consummation with love, as Maquokeeta takes his place in nature with Pocahontas, restores life to both the goddess and the poet. As the fertile winds blow over the land again, so too is the poet's vision restored: he senses the unseen power moving in him; and humbled by the beauty and terror of the experience, he closes with a prayer:

> We danced, O Brave, we danced beyond their farms,
> In cobalt desert closures made our vows . . .
> Now is the strong prayer folded in thine arms,
> The serpent with the eagle in the boughs.

The final union of time and space effected by the resurrecting dance is imaged in the harmonious coexistence of eagle and serpent. In a fleeting moment, the poet-dancer had touched hands with a life-giving, inviolable force and had sensed the possibility of renewal in the body of America. As Crane explained, he "had unlatched the door to the pure Indian world," and we are "led back in time to the pure savage world, while existing at the same time in the present," and knowing that in the ecstasy of the dance the twin realities become joined. But, as we shall discover, the tribal morn is only momentarily retrievable in dream; in "National Winter Garden" the dream of the poet Maquokeeta remains a mere debased vestige.

Consistently in "Powhatan's Daughter" Crane weights the role of the ritual dance in effecting the "mystical synthesis" that years later, in a small Mexican village, Taxco, he would experience in person. But the vision faltered. Nietzsche had written in *The Birth of Tragedy:*

> Every culture that has lost myth has lost, by the same token, its natural, healthy creativity, only a horizon ringed around with myths can unify a culture. . . . Man today, stripped of myth, stands famished among all his pasts and must dig frantically for roots, be it among the most remote antiquities.[32]

Hart Crane, like Whitman before him, wanted to forge the American myth, but either because America had lost its mythic sense or because of his personal tragedy, Crane's vision was dimmed. Or perhaps, as Eliot testified, to *sustain* that vision, "to apprehend/The point of intersection of the timeless/With time, is an occupation for the saint"; in any case, the remaining sections of *The Bridge* appear to document the darker side of America (except for "Atlantis"), a threnody of despair. Isadora's words which provide the epigraph to "Quaker Hill" are a reflection of Crane's own lost hope: "I see only the ideal. But no ideals have ever been fully successful on this earth."

"Indiana" signals the beginning of the dominance of images of the broken world that haunted Crane until his death. The vision of a unified world, in which real and ideal would be indissolubly wedded, became attentuated as little more than an echo of Whitman's dream. Lewis suggests that after "The Dance," action in *The Bridge* for the most part is a mere parody of earlier experiences. Pocahontas herself becomes the homeless squaw, "Perhaps a half-breed," her eyes "sharp with pain." Occasionally, in "Cutty Sark," moments of wine, laughter, and dance evoke our first, lost world, relieving the desultory scene too briefly:

> Then you may laugh and dance the axletree—
> Steel—silver—kick the traces—and know—

The modern nickelodeon world encroaches, dawn putting out the Statue of Liberty. The tempo of the mechanized city provides the music of "Cape Hatteras," but against Whitman's beating wand of song, its music is more the "thin squeaks of radio static"; its dance the swiftly wheeling planes dropping bombs, not the graceful gestures of the upward flight of ravens. The poet turns to Whitman, whose soaring voice relieves the death dance that is the wasteland world:

> Our Meistersinger, thou set breath in steel;
> And it was thou who on the boldest heel

> Stood up and flung the span on even wing
> Of that great Bridge, our Myth, whereof I sing!

The inspiration of Whitman—a remarkable one for Crane—is insufficient and the "gardenless Eve" that he seeks to recover in "Southern Cross" becomes the debased burlesque queen of "Winter Garden." The figure of Pocahontas is converted here into an image of eroticism without fulfillment, her dance a parody of spasms, obscene with no hint of beauty. Nonetheless, at the end, the stubborn aspiration prevails:

> Yet to the empty trapeze of your flesh,
> O Magdelene, each comes back to die alone
> Then you, the burlesque of our lust—and faith,
> Lug us back lifeward—bone by infant bone.

The dance disappears in the burlesque of faith, but not before the poet has invoked us to listen to the "one last angelus . . . Of pain that Emily, that Isadora knew!" The dance of life becomes a dance of death in the corrupted music of "The Tunnel":

> And somehow anyhow swing—
> The phonographs of hades in the brain
> Are tunnels that re-wind themselves, and love
> A burnt match skating in a urinal—
> Somewhere above Fourteenth TAKE THE EXPRESS
> To brush some new presentiment of pain—

Finally, "Atlantis" takes us back to the bright dream that kindled the creation of an American myth. The poem is Crane's last vision in *The Bridge*. Once more, the great bridge sustains his hope that has alternately ebbed and flowed throughout the poem. The power, grace, and beauty of the bridge are reinforced as he traces the upward flight of its cables:

Through the bound cable strands, the arching path
Upward, veering with light, the flight of strings,—
Taut miles of shuttling moonlight syncopate
The whispered rush, telepathy of wires.
Up the index of night, granite and steel—
Transparent meshes—fleckless the gleaming staves—
Sibylline voices flicker, wavering stream
As though a god were issue of the strings. . . .

The entire idiom of the poem is orchestral: the bridge's motion becomes a Psalm, a Choir, the Paradigm of a dancing god: "O Thou steeled Cognizance whose leap commits/The agile precincts of the lark's return," all of its gestures a ritual of transcendence. The bridge's "one song," "swift peals of secular life," lifts it beyond the tragic world and carries the poet along momentarily: "O Thou whose radiance doth inherit me," beyond time and space in "One Song, one Bridge of Fire!" The final image of the poem is one of rhythm and motion: "Whispers antiphonal in azure swing," a fitting close to a poem that began with the vision of the bridge as a reflection of God, the Primum Mobile. Although Crane's faith trembles in the tracing of his American dream, the poem, in these final lines, is an artistic refutation of that failure.

Looking back on Crane's brief poetic career and particularly at *The Bridge*, his whole artistic activity appears to have been an attempt to transcend the warring elements in his private life and to harmonize the "broken world" he saw around him with the perfected world he sensed within. He succeeded brilliantly, if sporadically, and some of his pride remained to the end in that accomplishment.

Vincent Quinn has observed that although Crane found life unbearable, he was a poet, a builder of words: "Writing poetry is an affirmation that precludes despair."[33] Hart Crane's personal tragedy, an almost total disorientation from the world at large, and his poetic tragedy, the inability to forge the Mexican myth, in no way eclipses the triumph of *The Bridge* or the poems that preceded and followed his "myth of America."

He never used the dance image again, not so much because it was an insufficient emblem of his vision, but because his vision failed. He ceased to think of "bridges." For Hart Crane, the dance had ended. But in the poetry he left behind, the vividness of his dance is etched with the indelibility of Portapovitch's own unforgettable art: "More real than life, the gestures you have spun/Haunt the blank stage with lingering alarms."

NOTES

1. Horton, *Hart Crane*, 1937, p. 143.
2. Jean D'Udine, *L'Art et le Geste*, in Susanne K. Langer, *Philosophy in a New Key* (Cambridge: Harvard University Press, 1943), p. 192.
3. Langer, p. 116.
4. Hart Crane, Letter to Gorham Munson, 17 March 1926, in *Complete Poems and Selected Letters*, ed. Weber, 1966, p. 227.
5. This and other letters included here in Unterecker, *Voyager*, 1969, p. 244.
6. Merce Cunningham, "Space, and Dance," *Modern Culture and the Arts*, eds. Hall and Ulanov, 1967, p. 348.
7. Angna Enters, "The Dance and Pantomime: Mimesis and Image," in *The Dance Has Many Faces*, ed. Sorell, 1951, p. 84.
8. Mary Wigman in Selden, *The Dancer's Quest*, 1935, p. 113.
9. "And Dancing is a moving all in measure," from Davies, "Orchestra," in *Poetry of the English Renaissance*, 1945, p. 338.
10. Jones, *Approach to the Purpose*, 1964, p. 10.
11. Unterecker, p. 284.
12. Crane, *Complete Poems*, p. 263.
13. These and other reminiscences of Crane in Unterecker.
14. Crane, *Complete Poems*, p. 217.
15. Trachtenberg, *Brooklyn Bridge*, 1966, p. 144.
16. Lewis, *The Poetry of Hart Crane*, 1962, p. 101.
17. Quoted by Langer in *Philosophy in a New Key*, p. 192.

18. Leibowitz, *Hart Crane*, 1968, p. 66.
19. Lewis, p. 104.
20. Leibowitz, pp. 66–69.
21. Lewis, p. 109.
22. Leibowitz, p. 68.
23. Dembo, *Conceptions of Reality*, 1968, p. 133.
24. Letter to Waldo Frank in Leibowitz, p. 70.
25. Dembo, p. 133.
26. Lewis, p. 118.
27. Unterecker, p. 276.
28. Ibid., p. 281.
29. Santayana, *Three Philosophical Poets*, 1938, p. 13.
30. Lewis, p. 311.
31. Letter to Otto Kahn in Horton, p. 338.
32. Nietzsche, *The Birth of Tragedy*, 1956, pp. 36–37.
33. Quinn, *Hart Crane*, 1963, p. 65.

CHAPTER IV

Dancing-Mad: Theodore Roethke

"The vision of the world as dancing people: my God, that is the world to come."

—T. Roethke

"Wait without thought, for you are not ready for thought; So the darkness shall be the light, and the stillness the dancing."

—T. S. Eliot

When Theodore Roethke, the "grass roots American with classic tastes," according to Bennington President Lewis Jones, arrived in Vermont in 1943 he brought with him boundless enthusiasm as well as a staggeringly ambitious syllabus for teaching "verse-writing." He wrote Allan Seager: "This place so far has astonished me."[1] The students soon adored him; the professional interchange was stimulating though "hysterical in some way."[2] But in the course of his visit, he came to know the economist Peter Drucker, the psychologist Eric Fromm, and the high priestess of modern dance, Martha Graham. Only recently, she expressed her art in terms Theodore Roethke would have found familiar then: "I take this puppet which was myself, and I fling it against the sky."[3] The happy coincidence of Graham's presence at Bennington at a time when American dance was enjoying great public attention could easily excite a beginning poet whose work was already suffused with dance images. In a career spanning thirty years, from the appearance in 1933 of "More Pure Than Flight" to "Once More the Round" composed less than two years before his death in 1963, Theodore Roethke was, by his own admission, "dancing-mad."

To trace the dance as an image in his poetry with its intricate and swift accretions of meaning is to follow the successive stages of Roethke's journey toward the discovery of the self. Martha Graham has called dance "the revelation of that inner landscape . . . which is a man's heart."[4] For Roethke, that "inner landscape" and the "outer landscape" of his father's greenhouse often converge into complex images of kinetic motion, often in the dance. At times, struggling "out of the slime" he is "crazed and graceless/A winter-leaping frog," or "the child of the dark," or a "one-legged man" who yearns to "out-leap the sun," willing himself to "place accurate feet upon the brink/Of nothingness." Responsive always to that inner cadence, "I hear my being dance from ear to ear," Theodore Roethke moved in his "slow spiritual progress" toward his "effort to be born."[5]

But the story of dance in his poetry is more than the account of the poet's pilgrimage of the soul—crucial as that is; it is testimony, as well, of the degree to which a complex and dynamic image was shaped into great and moving poetry. One of the distinguished pioneers of modern dance, Mary Wigman, wrote in 1963, "Dance is, like poetry and music, the intense concentration of uncountable oscillations striving toward one another in order to crystallize into a growing and molding of form."[6] Wigman postulates the problem both poet and dancer confronted when she asks the question Roethke asked all his life, "Does not the power, the magnificence of all creative art lie in knowing how to force chaos into form?"[7] Seeking a "new form" to express a network of inner experiences, Roethke wedded the dance to poetry as Yeats had done before him. He would fulfill the prophecy joyfully and boastfully set forth in a slight poem of his youth:

Someday I'll step with arrowed grace
Into the brighter realm of space:
. . . .
Before my patterned dance is done,
I'll pace on shadows to the sun.

"I am intoxicated with myself moving," Martha Graham had said.[8] For Theodore Roethke the same absorption imbued all of his poetry.

In an effort to assess Roethke's place in American poetry and to define limitations of his indebtedness to Wordsworth, Yeats, Whitman, and Eliot, critics agree that Roethke's "distinctive voice" emanates from his internal drama—the mind turned inward in search of the spirit, and his unique image of the "greenhouse Eden" which becomes the metaphor for a whole range of experiences. All of his poems converge around a few central themes which to a great degree ignore the world at large—politics, war, art, society in the aggregate, individual people. Unlike the poetry of Yeats, which heightens the tragedy of the Irish problem and eulogizes those fiery patriots Yeats loved and pitied and censured, Roethke's poetry seems oblivious to world problems. Emily Dickinson's breathless wonder at the prospects of an interior journey might well have guided Roethke's own:

Soto! Explore thyself
Therein thyself shall find
That undiscovered continent
No settler had the mind.

With the emergence of *The Lost Son & Other Poems* it became evident that Roethke would explore that "undiscovered continent" so that even the world of nature would become the correlative of his own loss, rediscovery, and rebirth. "Myself is what I wear:/I keep the spirit spare," he wrote in an early poem. Roethke's themes, growing out of his preoccupation with the self, reflect his absorption with "the canker at the root," his awareness of a dynamic life in even the humblest creatures around him, his need to summon up constantly the remembrance of things past in the Eden of his childhood, and his conviction that through intuition and the senses knowledge is gained that is otherwise denied the mind: "Sometimes the blood is privileged to guess/The things the eye or hand cannot possess."

Stephen Spender has described the progression of Roethke's themes from

> the child's absorption in the physical nature around him to confrontation with the polarity of people and things outside him—women, the woman!—and at the end of the separation of the spirit from the body, the confrontation with death. This development takes place before us like a very slow and awkward dance.[9]

Certainly, the poetry reveals a recurrent and persistent cycle of motifs, though not always as precise a "development" as Spender suggests. Frequently Roethke evokes his father's greenhouse—at once an admixture of the innocence, wonder, and beauty of growing things and the terror of the menacing, tenacious undergrowth—the slime in which the miraculous birth takes place. Papa, the bringer of order and light to the wildness of growing things, effects the fusion of opposites: the organic if chaotic process of being born with the artistic genius of the garden-god weeding, refining, patterning nature. But the theme of nature offers more to Roethke; it is also the reflection of the mysterious process within himself as *he* seeks his way out of loss, darkness, derangement, and death to light, awareness, birth, and transcendence. The diffusion of the separate self into the cosmic Oneness would be Roethke's route to the only form of immortality he could accept. Theodore Roethke could understand life ultimately as it related to death.

"To go forward as spiritual man, it is necessary to go back," Roethke observed, emphasizing the significance of rituals that evoke the primordial moment of sacred beginnings.[10] Roethke moves back not only to the innocence of his youth in his father's greenhouse world but to that first condition of man, to the beginnings in the floor of the sea. The immanent presence of the mythopoeic vision in Roethke links him naturally to the poets he most revered: Yeats, Whitman, and Eliot. He testifies both in his poetry and prose to the importance of the mythic view: "We live by fictions and myths. . . . They seem as necessary as food. If there is no God, we will invent one."[11] His notebooks reveal a lively interest in classic myths (he summarized endless numbers of them) and he knew well the work of Jung and modern mythographers, frequently referring to the impact of myth on the modern mind and citing Eliot's essay in the *Dial* on the need for the "mythical method" in modern poetry.

Several critics have noted the ritual movement attending Roethke's central themes. His compulsion to perform rites, akin to the sheer, inward need of primitive man, affirms Cassirer's conviction that "nature yields nothing without ceremonies."[12] Rituals in his poetry often celebrate, validate, and dramatize the "universal principle" of myth: the unity of all things in nature; they also serve to effect his passage from darkness to light, death to rebirth, and ignorance to knowledge in his larger quest of the soul for identity and eternity. At first charting his loss (Roethke has been called the "lost child" of modern poetry), he moves through a series of Protean transformations to celebration. If we recall that dance rituals in primitive societies abolished time, commemorated the mythic moment of beginning, identified the dancer-shaman with the gods, and marked the sacral seasons of cyclical life in nature and in man, we can appreciate the dance as a ritual of celebration in Roethke's poetry. Like those ancient ceremonies at Eleusis where sensual rites expressed the transcendent mysteries, Roethke's rituals are often erotic dances and hymns to the flesh, as the biological processes of fruition and birth in nature reflect the life-processes of man. If the journey to "God" can be effected only through the natural world of the senses, the perception of a universal Oneness is no less mystical. Coming to terms with mutability and decay by willing his own acceptance of the vitality extending infinitely in the universe and in the merest creature—indeed celebrating that process in endless rites— Roethke could triumph over his own annihilation.

Thus it becomes evident that Roethke's motifs—recovering the greenhouse, evoking the lost father, defining love through the erotic experience, returning to the beginnings in a succession of Protean transformations, seeking the stasis of the spirit in motion, confronting the "steady storm of correspondences" with both fear and bravado—are intrinsic to a quintessential spiritual quest: to measure and know himself. In this way, Cassirer tells us, man validates his own participation in a life-giving, inviolable force, a force most often symbolized in Roethke's poetry as motion, a dance. As we shall see, in each poem in which the dance appears, a microcosm of the search, the struggle, and the achievement of a "still point" is recapitulated. Like other American poets before him, Roethke would be a modern Siva: visionary like Whitman, shaman like Hart Crane, dancing bear and waltzing prophet, creating in poetry the patterned movements of rite and ceremony as an affirmation of the spirit.

The Dance Image in Roethke's Poetry

At its simplest level, the dance for Theodore Roethke was the dynamic movement of all living things, not the least of which was himself. Most reminiscences of Roethke consolidate around the single image of a great dancing bear. Roethke was a large man, perpetually in motion. His poetry reading is described by Stanley Kunitz: "Onstage . . . he clowned and hammed, incorrigibly, weaving, gyrating, dancing, shrugging his shoulders."[13] Blessing reports that "many a student seems to have been surprised to find his foot tapping in time to Roethke's bear-like professorial dance,"[14] and Spender remembers the "swaying, elephantine dance of his huge body."[15] In Seager's recollection, "he swung from side to side as he walked and his gait was often called 'bear-like.' "[16] In the only "moving picture" we have of him, David Myers's *In A Dark Time*,[17] Roethke sways and gestures and dances his way through the reading. Apparently, Roethke took to social dancing with gusto. He had learned to dance as a child of six in the Masonic Temple dance classes in Saginaw, and as an adult, if we believe May Kunkle, was quite a good social dancer.[18] Robert Heilman communicates some of the energy Roethke generated: "Eventually he would ease up himself and take the lead in genial noise, in guffawing, in frolicking fancies; and he loved to get a dance started. . . . At parties, I've heard women say, he was as good a dancer as he chose to be, light-footed and rhythmic."[19] Clearly, Roethke's own dancing made its way into the poetry. "In his poems," Spender observes, "Roethke seems often to be dancing. . . . It is simply Roethke incredibly and almost against his will dancing. He is the boy who is waltzed round by his father of the whiskeyed breath; the sensual man swaying toward the woman swaying toward him; the dying man dancing his way out of his body toward God. There was never, one might say, such ungainly yet compulsive dancing."[20]

The dancing bear is more than a *personal* emblem in Roethke's poetry. The motif is a familiar one in the history of recurrent symbols and conjures up a whole association of themes that enriches Roethke's use of the image. In the myth of Callisto, the unfortunate maiden is seduced by Zeus and changed into a bear when pursued by beasts. She is rescued and transformed by Zeus into a star, thus the origin of the twin constellations Ursa Major and Ursa Minor of the northern celestial hemisphere. The constellations compose an image of perfect harmony of motion in the heavens where the "dance of the stars" as Dante assures us reflects the "Glory of He who moves all things." The benign associations of the dancing bear are also traceable in the early rites of the corn spirit in most European and Asiatic cultures. The "Carnival Bear" of Shrovetide in the country districts of Bohemia danced in each household accompanied by joyous music and singing, and bestowed his benediction in the guise of a fertility god. Thus the restoration of the land was celebrated and commemorated by the dancing bear. If Flaubert in the nineteenth century knew of these myths, the irony posed by his juxtaposition of bears and stars is even more striking than the surface of the passage suggests, when he mourns that "human speech is like a cracked kettle on which we tap crude rhythms for bears to dance to, while we long to make music that will melt the stars."

In *Four for Sir John Davies* Roethke indirectly reminds us of the bear image Davies explores in "Orchestra":

> Thus when at first Love had them marshalled,
> as erst he did the shapeless mass of things,
> He taught them rounds and winding hay to tread,
> And about trees to cast themselves in rings;
> As the two Bears, whom the first mover flings
> With a short turn about heaven's axletree,
> In a round dance forever wheeling be.

Elsewhere, the uproarious antics of dancing bear of the circus, familiar to all of us as a symbol of absurdity seeking grace, are a poignant equation for our own frustrated and awkward reach for transcendence and beauty. At times in his poetry the bear symbolizes the imprisoned spirit in the flesh, so that after Roethke's death Myron Turner eulogized the poet who had

Raged and danced, danced and raged,
In what animal madness caught and caged.*

In Roethke's poetry the bear is a multifaceted image. Whether in "the slow/Wheel of stars, the Great Bear glittering colder than snow," he seems to "remember there was something else I was hoping for," or in the rudimentary, graceless steps of the primitive beast: "I circle on leather paws/In the darkening corridor," or in the joyfully capering circus creatures: "O watch his body sway!—/This animal remembering to be gay," Roethke's dancing bear connotes himself, man in general, and the indescribable mystery of the dancing stars.

Dance images in general in Roethke's poetry begin with the awareness of the cyclic activity in nature as all living things move in patterns of birth, death, and rebirth. As if hearing a rhythm subsumed in the hum of ordinary reality, the dancer celebrates the harmony intrinsic in the universe. Responding to the dance in nature, the poet often glimpses the stillness at the center of motion—observing, sensing, becoming a part of that dynamic motion himself. In these rare moments of revelation and transcendence, he both knows himself and is capable of losing himself, and his own dance becomes a ritual of dissolving into eternal things. All antitheses appear to melt into a universal dance: beginnings and endings, birth and death, stillness and motion are one and the same. As suggested earlier, in a large number of Roethke's poems, the process of "losing oneself" in another is dramatized in the erotic dance that sexual intercourse suggests. The Dionysian celebration of the flesh as a means of conquering time, death, and decay has a familiar echo in Elizabethan and metaphysical poetry, and for Roethke, especially, Davies's "Orchestra" and Marvell's invitation to his coy mistress strike the *carpe diem* motif with forceful power:

*Compare in John Berryman's dream poem: "On all fours he danced about his cage, poor Henry."

Now let us sport us while we may
And now, like amorous birds of prey,
Rather at once our time devour
Than languish in his slow-chapt power.
Let us roll all our strength and all
Our sweetness up into one ball,
And tear our pleasures with rough strife
Through the iron gates of life.

In all of Roethke's love poetry, the lover dances to the music of his pounding senses, and in the microcosm of his own birth, death, and rebirth in love confirms the process of conjunction all around him, like Eliot's dancers, "Keeping time,/Keeping the rhythm in their dancing/As in their living in the living seasons."

Finally the poet's dance is Art and Roethke unites himself, defying time and space, with others who have exerted themselves against the enemies—decay and annihilation—with Blake, Whitman, Yeats, and Eliot, all of whom he evokes through dance images:

Yes, I was dancing-mad, and how
That came to be the bears and Yeats would know.

The poet-dancer would know how to create multiple images of grace and order, and like Papa in the greenhouse, the consummate artist strives for "the imperishable quiet at the heart of form." Roethke knew the vulnerability, "The edge is what we have," and the possibility, "And everything comes to One,/As we dance on, dance on, dance on." The acceptance of both lies in delicate balance in his poetry. "Where's the bridge of dancing children?" he asked in one of his late poems. It would appear that for Theodore Roethke this quest never ceased.

The Poems

In 1933, in a poem little known by the public, Roethke expressed a theme that would persist in his later work: the portrait of the artist as dancer. First titled "More Pure Than Flight,"[21] this poetic sun-dance is interesting for both its cadenced rhythms and for the collage of images as the poet steps, treads, paces, walks, and dances his way out of the darkness into the light. "Someday I'll step with arrowed grace," he declares—defying time, space, death itself—as he seeks to become one with the natural movements of the cosmos. That he will surpass the flight of the curving bird has an unexpected echo in Hart Crane's own boast in *The Bridge* where the gull's "inviolate curve" is excelled by the great bridge's arc: "As though the sun took step of Thee, yet left/ Some motion ever unspent in thy stride." Roethke never included "Someday I'll Step" (the poem's later title) in any volume of his poetry, yet it is noteworthy for the motifs that would recur in his mature poems: the "brink of nothingness," the fear of his own annihilation, and the exuberant defiance: "Death shall not drift my limbs apart/When ancient silence storms my heart." The poem reminds us too of Eliot's early enactment of the ritual dance in "The Death of Saint Narcissus": "So he became a dancer before God." Although the tone of Eliot's poem of martyrdom differs, both poets in their youth created poems in which the dance as a ritual of transcendence is transformed for their special uses into a celebration of the self.

The poems that compose *Open House*, Roethke's first published volume, testify to an order, a harmony in nature which the poet apprehends but can seldom penetrate. Walking will become transformed ultimately to dancing. "Walking this field" he remembers the innocence of childhood when he tried to match his father's stride. Now, walking "on a treeless plain,/With ankles bruised from stubble of the grain," he confesses he's lost: "We walk unaware of what is far or close."

The world first recognized Theodore Roethke in 1948 with the publication of *The Lost Son And Other Poems*. In the short pieces that serve as a prelude to the theme of the "lost child," we are carried backward in time for minutely detailed evocations of the greenhouse Eden—that microcosm of subterranean nature where things grow out of the slime and flourish under Papa's planting, pinching, coaxing, watering, weeding, cutting: "all night watering roses, his feet blue in rubber boots." Death and life coexist comfortably in the long greenhouse world. We glimpse the small boy "crawling on all fours/Alive in a slippery grave," or standing precariously atop the greenhouse roof: "My feet crackling splinters of glass and dried putty/And everyone pointing and shouting." As in *Open House*, the need to find his own "footing" is a pervasive theme in Roethke's poetry. In "My Papa's Waltz," the small boy clings dizzily to his father as he is whirled round and round in an exuberant celebration of love. Roethke had written in his high school story "Papa" that the boy "put his feet on top of Papa's and they'd waltz." Here is the poem: the image of Papa with his whiskeyed breath, his knuckles battered, his palm caked with the dirt of the roses, beating time on the head of the adoring child, not only a silhouette of Papa's energy and motion—it is *his* waltz—but also sufficient testimony of the child's difficulty in dancing alone: "I hung on like death/Such waltzing is not easy." As he is whirled off to bed by the doting father, basking in the warmth of his affection, we sense too the poignancy of the man in the present—bereft of all that Papa symbolized: order, strength, harmony, and love. As late as 1963, the year of his death, Roethke would be haunted by that loss and the world Otto represented, and he could still evoke with Wordsworthian longing that unredeemable first world:

In my mind's eye I see those fields of glass,
As I looked out at them from the high house,
Riding beneath the moon, hid from the moon,

Then slowly breaking whiter in the dawn;
When George the watchman's lantern dropped from sight
The long pipes knocked: it was the end of night.
I'd stand upon my bed, a sleepless child
Watching the waking of my father's world,—
O world so far away! O my lost world!

In many respects "My Papa's Waltz"—a poem that has enjoyed universal popularity—is a rite of love that Roethke sought to repeat all his life in his poetry: that great, awkward moving body recreating the joy of childhood. Those who attended Roethke's reading of this his favorite poem always described his undulating body as a dance.

"The Long Alley" opens with the images that recapitulate the patterns of darkness and light, death and rebirth that mark the entire quartet of "The Lost Son." The dead, coaxed into the dance that constitutes the entire third section, are spirits from a buoyant, meaningful past, the Elizabethan Age: "A waiting ghost warms up the dead/Until they creak their knees." The song-and-dance rhythms, the nonsense rhymes, the English gilliflowers, the energetic Renaissance tone evoke another golden time, an age when men and women danced, as Eliot had recalled in the words of his famous ancestor, Sir Thomas Elyot, in "necessarye coniunction." This faint echo from the past produces the "minor ecstasy" at the end of the poem when, coming out of the shade, "the long alleys of string and stem," into the "soft light," the speaker notices for the first time the flowers "swaying over the walks," their "petals pulsing."

So in "A Field of Light," as the title suggests, the lost child begins to sense "the separateness of all things."

> Alone, I kissed the skin of a stone;
> Marrow-soft, danced in the sand.

The dance here is a quiet ritual celebration for the awareness he has momentarily experienced. Suddenly, he is privy to the path walking, the sun glittering, the elm filling with birds, the lark singing, the salt laughing. Awakened to the miracle of harmonious nature, he stands strong and confident; if only for an evanescent moment he has found his footing and can walk *with* nature:

> And I walked, I walked through the light air;
> I moved with the morning.

Having journeyed through the stages of stagnation, confused action, observation, and growing awareness to the "mild dance" at the close of the experience, he has, in Roethke's own gloss, achieved light at a cost, and his "heart lifted up with the great grasses."

In the last poem of the series, "The Shape of the Fire," the death-life paradox is dramatized in the "storm of correspondences" contained in this final experience of disorientation and apprehension. The dance, usually signifying birth, "Mother me out of here," is more a *danse macabre*, an initiation into the dread darkness: "These flowers are all fangs. Comfort me, fury./Wake me, witch, we'll do the dance of rotten sticks." Death has become a necessary prefiguration of life as reiterated in the cycles in nature and ultimately in the experience of the speaker. He discovers that "in the hour of ripeness the tree is barren." The eye that should see anew, the ear that should hear, the shoe that could waltz the way to renewal are missing! Instead, for the awkward quester, there is "only one shoe/For the Waltz of To,/The pinch of Where." Comprehending little more than that "the journey from flesh is longest," the lost son discovers "the redeemer comes a dark way." Retreating further into that "minnowy world of weeds and ditches," he begins to experience the first small breath of life. The last passage of "The Shape of the Fire" is a climax of affirmation after the experience of the *danse macabre* and the nightmare of dreaded oblivion.

Beatrice Roethke notes that the sequence of the "lost son"

poems was meant to include Part Two of "Praise to the End" and "O, Thou Opening, O" and the two do indeed pick up the quest for the lost Eden and are consistent in tone with the quartet. The speaker, seeking himself in the refractory light of memory though lost in the dark wood—a Dantean echo—romps "down the summery streets of my veins." Like Eliot's children "singing in the cupola," the jingle of the childish voices as they dance has a ghostly, unreal quality. "What footie does is final" has some of the eeriness of a graveside *danse macabre*, and the speaker awakes to find he's been "asleep in a bower of dead skin" and the dreams have been ritual patterns of death and birth. He wakes to *awareness*, a familiar metaphor in Roethke's poetry, for the darkness has revealed not only the sea-faced uncles but himself: "The dark showed me a face." Punning on the mystical experience of *becoming*, Roethke concludes, "The light becomes me." As forecast in the opening lines of the poem, "Bumpkin, he can dance alone" (an echo of Mother Goose's "Dance, Thumbkin, Dance"), the dance in "Praise to the End" is neither mad nor erotic—as it will become in later poems. Here, it is an evocative image of that first world, revealing to the sorrowing and lost grown man the route to transcendence: "I lost my identity to a pebble;/The minnows love me, and the humped and spitting creatures./I believe!—"

"I'll make it," he asserts confidently in "O, Thou Opening, O": "I'll change the image, and my shoes." But the preparation for the new image is prefigured in "Unfold! Unfold!" which marks another occasion in Roethke's lonely journey to self-discovery. "I ache for another choice," he says there; and the motion of expanding outward, "I stretched like a board, almost a tree," and the dance in the simple wood culminate in the poems that follow: the search for the self in a woman. The toad waltzing on a drum and the "king of boops"— Roethke's eternal mockery of himself as a lover—still cry hopefully for love, musing, "we never enter/Alone." So it is in "O, Thou Opening, O," he casts off the "ghostly going of tame bears," the "dance of dead underwear, or the sad waltz of paper bags"—all images of the futility of his "spiritual pigrimage": "Who ever said God sang in your fat shape?" and commits himself instead to sensual fulfillment. The ironic, self-derisive tone disappears totally as the poem expands into a wildly erotic Dionysian dance of joy. He asks in wondrous disbelief, "You mean?—/I can leap, true to the field,/In the lily's sovereign right?/Be a body lighted with love?" He sways and dances "like a sapling tree," and sings "the green and things to come." The verbs convey the new sense of felt life: leaping, swaying, singing, twinkling. Roethke amuses himself with metaphysical puns, "So alive I could die," and finally *seeking* and *seeing* in the same instant concludes, "Going is knowing." His final lines, an invitation to the revelations of the flesh, is a prelude to the climactic dancing in "Four For Sir John Davies": "Be true,/Skin."

"I've done some poems on dancing,"[22] Roethke wrote casually to Kenneth Burke in 1952, adding little more save that they would appear in *The Atlantic* and *Poetry Review* that fall. Thus the first two parts of his fine dance quartet made a somewhat unpretentious appearance. "The Dance" and "The Partner"—eventually to be part of "Four For Sir John Davies"—were instantly acclaimed, to Roethke's surprise, by Dylan Thomas and W. H. Auden. Pleased, he wrote to Peter Viereck, "Auden startled me by his enthusiasm for them,"[23] and similarly to Arabel Porter, "Thomas . . . thought those dancing pieces wonderfully good!"[24]

The four poems, completed by "The Wraith" and "The Vigil" that same year, represent Roethke at the height of his powers: his assured control of form in the "modified" *rime royal*, the richness of the dance image as he explores its symbolic planes, and the mature expression of a theme that had engaged his thoughts for twenty years: the defeat of time through a revelation of the self. The formula had already been sketched in "The Lost Son": to find himself, he must first lose himself.

His quest earlier had been in the nostalgic evocation of the long greenhouse and Papa's world—in memory. Now, in a passionate sexual union, he would "lose himself" again and again in woman, seeking and finding in each dissolution of the self a triumph over isolation, change, and death. Here, momentarily, the lovers "undid chaos with a curious* sound." As we shall see in Roethke's last poems, even this would prove insufficient as he moved irrevocably to the realization that only by dissolving into the cosmos, the earth itself, could he achieve apotheosis. But in "Four for Sir John Davies," in the Elizabethan *carpe diem* motif, Roethke could explore immortality. And like Donne and Davies and Marvell, he would measure himself, not so much by other men, as by the universe itself.

Roethke's inspiration, as he tells us, came from Sir John Davies's unfinished poem, "Orchestra," an invitation to make love, expressed in the metaphor of dancing as part of the cosmos in which all things move in divinely orchestrated unison. Written in 1594, Davies's poem begins with an invocation to the Muse of Dance, Terpsichore, to inspire the poet's epic retelling of Antinous's wooing of Penelope, who awaits the return of Ulysses from the Trojan wars. In many respects, the poem heralds the new voice we associate with the Metaphysical school of poetry, a love epic that eschews sentiment, modesty, and decoration for wit, humor, and sophistry. Antinous, pleading with Penelope to dance and love, prefigures Marvell's shrewd and witty lover in "To His Coy Mistress" in his mental agility, his worldliness, and his genius for conceiving a network of images for the irrefutable rhythm of life. The theme is an old Elizabethan touchstone, but the voice is new: energetic, intelligent, and irresistibly eloquent. It is in the tradition of the poetry of ideas, and its amusing "Argument" is not to be denied.

Curious, as Denis Donoghue reminds us, means careful as well as strange and exploratory. See Denis Donoghue, "Roethke's Broken Music," in Stein, p. 143.

Antinous's thesis is deceivingly artless: The whole universe dances, why not they? As he woos Penelope, he envisions all cosmic movement from Creation onward as a dance:

> Dancing, bright lady, then began to be
> When the first seeds whereof the world did spring,
> The fire, air, earth, and water did agree
> By Love's persuasion, nature's mighty king,
> To leave their first disordered combating,
>   And in a dance such measure to observe
>   As all the world their motion should preserve.

Defining his term, "Dancing is a moving all in measure," Antinous argues that all disparate elements in nature are fused by harmonious movement, a pattern reflecting the mind of the Primum Mobile itself. Thus man finds *his* significance in becoming part of divine will. Dancing is "love's proper exercise" wherein man makes his compromise with Time "the measure of all moving." The argument reminds us of Marvell's triumphant conclusion: "Thus, though we cannot make our sun/Stand still, yet we will make him run."

Davies assimilates in "Orchestra" every symbolic configuration dance had suggested in the sixteenth century and more—from the purely physical motion of all living things, to the primitive and ritualistic, to the erotic, and ultimately to the transcendental. Dancing is the endless movement of converging elements, the essence of the circling galaxies:

> The turning vault of heaven formed was,
> Whose starry wheels he hath so made to pass
> As that their movings do a music frame
> And they themselves still dance unto the same.

Dance was "born" when Time itself came into being: "When outleaped Dancing from the heap of things/And lightly rode upon his nimble wings." The world took its name from

"whirling" in a dance, and Antinous pictures Earth as a fe-
cund woman who appears to be still but whose orbiting
center is complemented by the movement of her waters and
roadways. Meander's path dances as do the streams, the
flowers waving in the wind, the vines circling round the elm
tree, the birds in flight, even "Chance herself her nimble feet
upbears/On a round slippery wheel, that rolleth aye,/And
turns all states with her impetuous way."

Antinous summons up all the gods: Bacchus, Venus,
Mars, Vulcan, and the Muses who dance to please Jove—the
first and greatest dancing god of all. Having presented an
inexhaustible vision of a dancing universe, Antinous triumphantly enjoins Penelope's court:

> Learn then to dance, you that are princes born
> And lawful lords of earthly creatures all;
> Imitate them, and thereof take no scorn,
> For this new art to them is natural.
> And imitate the stars celestial,
>> For when pale death your vital twist shall sever,
>> Your better parts must dance with them forever.

Calling up the specter of the dreaded *danse macabre*, Penelope's convincing lover reminds her, "Love danceth in
your pulse and in your veins," for "thus Love persuades."
That the microcosm and the macrocosm move in concentric
rhythms that surpass the merely sensual is Antinous's most
convincing appeal:

> Lo, this is Dancing's true nobility:
> Dancing, the child of Music and of Love;
> Dancing itself, both love and harmony,
> Where all agree and all in order move;
> Dancing, the art that all arts do approve;
> The fair character of the world's consent,
> The heav'n's true figure, and the earth's ornament.

Davies's poem, a *rime royal* pattern of seven lines in iambic pentameter with a rhyme scheme of *ababbcc*, is itself a reflection of the order and harmony he offers temptingly to the resisting Penelope. The final triumph of "Orchestra" is the conviction that poetry, like dance, is "th'only perfect plea-sure/That wretched earth-born men have ever known." The concord, grace, and patterned beauty Davies reveals is his own response to the turbulent Elizabethan world:

> And in my mind such sacred fury move,
> As I should knock at heav'n's great gate above
>   With my proud rhymes; while of this heav'nly state
>   I do aspire the shadows to relate.

More than any of his Elizabethan contemporaries, Sir John Davies was the quintessential poet as dancer.

Theodore Roethke's title, "Four For Sir John Davies," is first a tribute to an inspiring predecessor who, like himself, saw all natural movement as a microcosmic dance of celebration; secondly, the poem forges a link with the past whose significance Roethke so keenly felt. Much like Pound, who merges with Waller's dust: "Siftings on siftings in oblivion,/Till change hath broken down/All things save Beauty alone," Roethke merges with the Elizabethan poet who also needed "a place to sing and dancing-room." Roethke's own four dances become the correlative for his changing inner states: joyful elation, madness, passion, and spiritual yearning. Adapting Davies's stanza to a six-line iambic pentameter pattern with a rhyme scheme of *ababcc*, replete with anapests that create the dance measures of the lines, Roethke consciously fuses form and substance.

Part I, "The Dance," seems almost a continuation of the speculative, objective detachment that so often initiates a poem in the Metaphysical mode:

> Is that dance slowing in the mind of man
> That made him think the universe could hum?

112

The great wheel turns its axle when it can,
I need a place to sing, and dancing-room,
And I have made a promise to my ears
I'll sing and whistle romping with the bears.

For they are all my friends: I saw one slide
Down a steep hillside on a cake of ice,—
Or was that in a book? I think with pride:
A caged bear rarely does the same thing twice
In the same way: O watch his body sway!—
This animal remembering to be gay.

I tried to fling my shadow at the moon,
The while my blood leaped with a wordless song.
Though dancing needs a master, I had none
To teach my toes to listen to my tongue.
But what I learned there, dancing all alone,
Was not the joyless motion of a stone.

I take this cadence from a man named Yeats;
I take it, and I give it back again:
For other tunes and other wanton beats
Have tossed my heart, and fiddled through my brain.
Yes, I was dancing-mad, and how
That came to be the bears and Yeats would know.

The opening restraint and objectivity are, of course, short-lived. Having posed Wordsworth's great theme, "Little we see in Nature that is ours," and having contemplated the irrevocable turning of the universal wheel, the speaker moves away to focus on the subjective ego—the true object of his intense concern. His compulsion to dance and sing and link himself with meaningful activity seems to balance the fear that the dance is "slowing in the mind of man"; in reality, his own internal rhythm beating in his ears urges him to "sing and whistle" and romp with the bears. Roethke is again the dancing bear but he is also the artist, obsessed with the need to express himself: "I need a place to sing, and dancing-room." The choice of words is crucial: each term for dance becomes interchangeable with the creative act of writing poetry: romping, flinging, swaying, dancing-mad. The comic and cosmic dimensions of the bears are offered simultaneously here: awkward yet capering, all Roethke's bears converge in a singularly ironic image of the imprisoned flesh. Like the tramps waiting for Godot, the bears pass the time in "play," inventing and reinventing their dance. In the familiar metamorphosis we have come to expect in Roethke, the poet merges with the bears: he *is* the caged bear who sways; he *is* "this animal remembering to be gay." This second stanza is highly reminiscent too of Frost's reflective mode, the pleasant ease with which he first observes the creatures in nature who become the occasion for his own inner confrontation. As the shift occurs from a quiet tone to one of more intense excitation, the quickening momentum is felt in the verbs which move from seeing and thinking to flinging and leaping. The sheer effort of that impossible aspiration, "I tried to fling my shadow at the moon," can be contrasted with Roethke's youthful boast, "Someday I'll step with arrowed grace/Into the brighter realm of space." Here, alone, untutored, aided by little more than the intuitive message from the blood—the wordless song—he learns nonetheless. Longing to express the inexpressible through gesture, he *is* more than stone, his joy the residue of the attempted flight upward. The final stanza of "The Dance" conjures up not only the imprisoned bears' defiant, artful, and innovative dance and Yeats's Byzantium "where blood-begotten spirits come/And all complexities of fury leave,/Dying into a dance"; it asserts, as well, what the poet learned "dancing all alone," heeding the tunes and beats tossing his heart and fiddling through his brain. The poem ends with confession and anticipation, a glimmering of the experience to come in "The Partner":

> Yes, I was dancing-mad, and how
> That came to be the bears and Yeats would know.

The tension in "The Dance" derives from the fine balance of antitheses, the hallmark of Roethke's most successful poems. Here are the juxtaposition of fast and slow rhythms; the inexorable moving of the spheres and his own mad dancing; detached speculation and subjective searching; past and present; animal, human, and cosmic imaged in the romping bears, the lonely artist, and the purgatorial trials of Yeats's spirits. "The Dance" serves to initiate the central antithesis of the quartet, the opposite of sensual and spiritual perfectly balanced in the following three poems whose paradox and ambiguities will be resolved finally in the poem that follows, "The Waking."

As we have seen in this first poem of the quartet, the dance has undergone a subtle accretion of meaning. From the circling spheres and the swaying bears to the speaker's own upward reach toward the moon, to the ghostly agonies of Byzantium, and finally to the poet's dancing madness, the dance has evoked both sensual and transcendent nuances. Significantly, the drama has been played out in the mind. From "the dance slówing in the mind of man" in the opening lines to the tunes and beats that fiddle through the brain, the poem comes full circle as an inward experience. The poet is alone—listening to the cosmic music, recalling the bears sliding on the ice (he's not even sure he *saw* the bears! "Or was that in a book?"), feeling the blood pounding in his veins, but always *alone*.

Conversely, "The Partner," the next experience in the search for the self, is one of sensual desire that first perplexes and then exhilarates. The erotic dance prefigures not only the consummation of the lovers but the union of flesh and spirit as well. The whole of this second poem is a sexual rite danced against the macabre backdrop of "that dark world"—death. The chiaroscuro effect is achieved by the startling juxtapositions that create the fundamental tensions of the poem: animal with human, darkness with light, acceleration and action with lassitude and inertia, flesh with spirit, life with death.

We played a measure with commingled feet:
The lively dead had taught us to be fond.

The sheer sexual abandon of the lovers achieving climax is complemented in the living, breathing activity around them: "Light altered light along the living ground." The heron prances, the elephants dance, "the living all assemble," enfolding the lovers in their company. Revealing a logic of its own, the sensual experience contains the essence of something more: "We live beyond/Our outer skin," and ultimately both body and soul "know how to play/In that dark world where gods have lost their way." The indivisible unity of sense and spirit as fit contestant against the darkness of death and annihilation is an old theme. Marvell's lovers were impelled by the chill of the grave, "But at my back I always hear,/Time's winged chariot hurrying near." Even Eliot's quester, after witnessing the "seduction" of the typist in *The Waste Land*, has a faint intimation of Ferdinand's joy on hearing Ariel's celebration of survival, "This music crept by me upon the waters." What Roethke does hear, absent in Eliot's poem, is Ferdinand's affirmation that the music "allays both their fury and my passion with its sweet air." Roethke's subtle evocation of both *The Tempest* and *The Waste Land*, "O what lewd music crept into our ears!" reinforces the joy and fulfillment of this erotic dance at a time when the spirit was indeed wasted.

The theme of love is continued in "The Wraith" where again the polar emotions of "gaiety and dread" are juxtaposed. "The spirit and the flesh cried out for more," against the spectral warning of the dead.

We two, together, on a darkening day
Took arms against our own obscurity.

Reinforcing the theme, that love *is* the answer to time and death, the poet learns that finding the self is the corollary of losing the self: each lover *becomes* the other. If only momentarily, they fuse into an indivisible oneness, transcend their own flesh, and like the miraculous angels can dance on a pin, finding light and love in the darkness itself:

> The flesh can make the spirit visible:
> We woke to find the moonlight on our toes.

The movement in the entire poem from darkness to light, from sleeping to waking (always *awareness* in Roethke's poetry), from death to life is traceable through the sexual experience. The poem in its rhythms and gestures constitutes a twin image of dance and act of love. But it is also the commerce of the body and soul, a neo-Platonic transformation in which the souls prevail: "Our souls looked forth, and the great day stood still." The poem concludes with a beautiful image of a perfected experience. As the lovers, united, rise to meet the moon in a soaring climax of movement, the moon descends slowly to meet them. Measuring their love in cosmic terms, finding the perfect execution of a dance shared by lovers and the moon, the poet achieves a stasis of surpassing harmony. The intimation of death in the final image of the moon, "Impaled on light, and whirling slowly down," carries not only the double entendre—dying as sexual climax in Renaissance poetry—but also prefigures the experience of the final poem.

A vigil is an "awaiting," and the last poem of "Four for Sir John Davies" finds the poet, like another quester in the past, awaiting his own immortality. Purgatory itself is an experience of the souls circling upward through trial and suffering awaiting the joy of expiation and the triumphant entry into Paradise. Dante's vision of the perfection of "the mighty power beyond his will," conveyed through the celestial guidance of Beatrice at the Virgin's request, comes, if we recall, only after his own purgation of lust in the "refining fire." Awed and trembling at the summit of Purgatory, Dante beholds the fulfilled vision: the heavenly procession and the flawless beauty of Beatrice. Transformed by love himself, Roethke's Dante shares his experience with the poet and all lovers:

> All lovers live by longing, and endure:
> Summon a vision, and declare it pure.

Like Dante, the speaker of "The Vigil" is also poet and lover, seeker of "the hidden virtue without flaw," through an experience of the senses and the spirit. Inspired by the reminder of Dante's vision, he turns back to *his* love, to *his* voyage through death to rebirth. Like Dante, his experience of illumination comes with awareness. "Did Beatrice deny what Dante saw?" Seeing is perceiving, as we know in both Dante's poetry and Roethke's. In a final poem before his death, Roethke would write, "I embrace what I perceive!/Brothers and sisters, dance ye/Dance ye all!"

"The Vigil," like the poems preceding it, is a dance, but the solo celebration of the self and the subsequent erotic dance become now a significant ritual of passage from death to life. Moving from chaos to unity and harmony ("We undid chaos with a curious sound"), from darkness to light as night becomes morning ("We dared the dark to reach the white and warm."), from life to death to rebirth ("Alive at noon, I perished in her form."), the dance brings the lovers finally from flesh to spirit, inspiring poetry itself:

> Who rise from flesh to spirit know the fall:
> The word outleaps the world, and light is all.

As in the earlier poems, the sexual joy of the lovers is set against darkness and death:

> We danced to shining; mocked before the black
> And shapeless night that made not answer back.

118

Their reality emanates not from the visible world—hostile and chaotic—but from themselves in the experience of rapture, movement, oneness. The final lines testify to the transformation the lovers achieve because, like Marvell's lovers, they "dared." Thus at the close of "Four for Sir John Davies" that paradox—the experience of losing oneself in another to gain oneself—is one costing, as Eliot said, "not less than everything." As "The Vigil" closes the quartet, all antitheses coalesce in a final affirmation of the power of love in an indifferent world. Roethke touches on a theme that will persist in the final poems: all death is life, and the fall into unconsciousness—here in sexual dissolution—is the only immortality we can know. This is what awareness has yielded up. His word upon this truth *outleaps* the world, the final image of the poem one of vital motion. Eliot's observation in "Burnt Norton" is a fitting gloss on Roethke's own quartets: "The detail of the pattern is movement."

"The Waking," which immediately follows "Four for Sir John Davies," is the culmination of the preceding experiences. The speaker's voice is calm and measured; in fact the entire poem moves in deliberate patterned rhythms. The theme grows out of paradox: waking through sleep, knowing through sensation, stasis after movement:

> We think by feeling. What is there to know?
> I hear my being dance from ear to ear.
> I wake to sleep, and take my waking slow.

Awaking becomes the metaphor for awareness, knowledge, acceptance. The activity of the poem is a kind of slow dance as the verbs move from waking to going, to walking softly, to climbing, to shaking, and finally to falling away. "What falls is always" is the wisdom imparted in the process of learning by "going where to go." The rhymes which fuse *slow* with *know* and *go* serve to dissolve the antitheses posed and enhance the remarkably quiet tone. The unalterable necessity of accepting finally that which is beyond reason and is felt only intuitively is as close as Roethke ever comes to stoicism. Many more times, he will fall into the abyss, caper like a crazed bear, search the spirit for the answer, "How to be?" but here in the final poem of "Praise to the End" Theodore Roethke tunes in, as nowhere else, to the music of his internal dance.

Words For The Wind, published in 1958, recapitulates the themes and motifs that recur from the beginning: the confrontation with death and the self, and the search for harmonizing motion. Yeats and Eliot still echo in the "Meditations of an Old Woman" with its reflective tone, its preoccupation with age and unfulfillment, and the central image of the archetypal journey. But the voice of *Words* is new and sure, exuberant and hopeful—no doubt the result of both Roethke's successful reception during his travels in Europe on a Fulbright Fellowship and the five years of his very happy marriage to Beatrice. The stark gravity of Roethke's persistent themes is leavened with whimsy and self-parody: "And I danced round and round,/A fond and foolish man." The rhythms are free and often soaring. Here is Roethke at the summit of his power as a poet and his optimism as a man. *Words For The Wind*, which includes a series of sprightly rhymes for children, is a dance of life, much as the posthumously published *The Far Field* is a dance of death. Again love and motion are equated, and as in "John Davies" that movement is a ritual of physical love. As Blessing notes, "The dance of energy is the same for the atoms and amoebae, for the sun flowers and for rodents, for human beings, for the galaxy, for the universe itself."[25]

In both "The Dream"—an airy, delicate wish-fulfillment— and in "Words for the Wind," which gives its title to the collection, loving is a "flowing" together, a changing, cadenced series of patterned movements, a dance. Here the woman ("She knew the grammar of least motion") instructs the poet in the art of love:

I watched her there, between me and the moon;
The bushes and the stones danced on and on;
I touched her shadow when the light delayed;
· ·
She held her body steady in the wind;
Our shadows met, and slowly swung around;
She turned the field into a glittering sea;
I played in flame and water like a boy
And I swayed out beyond the white seafoam;
Like a wet log, I sang within a flame.
In that last while, eternity's confine,
I came to love, I came into my own.

The power of the lovers to transfigure the elements, who—
in Donne's vision—"did the whole world's soul contract,"
here becomes the defiant answer to "eternity's confine." Later, in "Words for the Wind," the poet testifies, "All's even
with the odd," for the dance of the lovers is a triumph of
accord, conveyed in the sexual act. "She sways whenever I
sway." The tempo in "Words for the Wind" quickens with
verbs of leaping, moving, rising, swinging, and falling, and
climaxes finally with the woman frolicking "like a beast" and
the poet-lover dancing round and round as he can "see and
suffer myself/In another being at last."

Perhaps the most delightful contribution to *Words For The
Wind*, and surely the best-known of Roethke's poems, is "I
Knew A Woman." The movements of the woman rehearse
the stages of the Greek ode—originally danced—in which
the singers move up in one direction during the *strophe*,
move down the other during the *antistrophe*, and stand in
place during the *epode*: "She taught me Turn, and Counter-
turn, and Stand." As we examine the poem, several dance
motifs are immediately apparent:

I knew a woman, lovely in her bones,
When small birds sighed, she would sigh back at them;

121

Ah, when she moved, she moved more ways than one:
The shapes a bright container can contain!
Of her choice virtues only gods should speak,
Or English poets who grew up on Greek
(I'd have them sing in chorus, cheek to cheek).

How well her wishes went! She stroked my chin,
She taught me Turn, and Counter-turn, and Stand;
She taught me Touch, that undulant white skin;
I nibbled meekly from her proffered hand;
She was the sickle; I, poor I, the rake,
Coming behind her for her pretty sake
(But what prodigious mowing we did make).

Love likes a gander, and adores a goose:
Her full lips pursed, the errant note to seize;
She played it quick, she played it light and loose;
My eyes, they dazzled at her flowing knees;
Her several parts could keep a pure repose,
Or one hip quiver with a mobile nose
(She moved in circles, and those circles moved).

Let seed be grass, and grass turn into hay:
I'm martyr to a motion not my own;
What's freedom for? To know eternity.
I swear she cast a shadow white as stone.
But who would count eternity in days?
These old bones live to learn her wanton ways:
(I measure time by how a body sways).

Like the woman herself, the poem "moves" from Greek ode,
controlled and stylized, to freedom and abandoned play as
the lovers dance toward each other, and finally to the stasis of
the speaker's closing reflection. The woman is all seductive
movement but various and mysterious, the bright container
of mercurial shapes. Both goddess and wanton, she penetrates some universal truth, evoking the answering sighs of

the birds and the reflex of universal motion: "She moved in circles, and those circles moved." On one level, the dance is sheer sex play—the "prodigious mowing" is Roethke at his bawdy best—but on another level, it is an intimation of immortality. In joining her dance, he becomes her martyr, but he also glimpses eternity. The final line, "I measure time by how a body sways," is Roethke's triumphant fusion of all the poem's ambiguities and extravagant double entendre. Through an art that both engages and transcends time and space, here a ritual dance of love, he solves the dilemma of his own ephemeral state and comes to accept the necessity of cyclical birth, life, and death. "Let seed be grass, and grass turn into hay" mirrors back, in the singular verb, the *turning* of the lovers to each other. Much in the manner of Marvell's own lovers, they have defeated time. The tone is also Marvell's: humorous with undertones of seriousness and reflection, playful and engaging, sophisticated and ingenuous. The fundamental opposition of motion and stasis is worked out with subtlety in the repetitions and the constant juxtapositions of images of repose and movement, much like the modern dancer whose pauses are as weighted with meaning as her leaps and falls.

Other love poems in *Words For The Wind* play on these familiar motifs: the harmony in "She" between the woman and the birds; the sacral union of the lovers singing and dancing together; the joyous exultation as nature joins their celebration; and the recurrent activity of dancing, moving, flowing, romping, and circling their way through life:

> The garden is a river flowing south.
> She cries out loud the soul's own secret joy;
> She dances, and the ground bears her away.
> ....
> She moves as water moves, and comes to me,
> Stayed by what was, and pulled by what would be.

The final line with its reference to the relentlessness of the
tides' ebb and flow parallels the inescapability of the sexual
union. But even more, it signals the lover's own destiny. "Is
she what I become?" he had asked in "The Other," and the
answer is offered in "The Sententious Man": "Each one's
himself, yet each one's everyone." Searching for a rebirth of
the soul, in "The Renewal" he asks, "Will the self, lost, be
found again?" and finding love, he can discover, "I am everywhere." Thus, at a critical stage of Roethke's development,
despite the intermittent periods of desperation and despair,
the "perpetual affirmations" come as a response to the
woman's invitation:

> She lilts a low soft language, and I hear
> Down long sea-chambers of the inner ear.

In these poems, as in many of Donne's love lyrics, the individual experience is measured against the cosmos, lifting the
lovers into that significant and universal dimension.

"The Dying Man" marks a subtle shift in Roethke's vision;
the spirit and tone are reminiscent of Yeats in the Byzantium
poems—the poem dedicated to the older Yeats whose heart
too swayed with the world but longed for the release from
time and change. Here the poet is "that final thing,/A man
learning to sing." The argument of the poem is an extension
of earlier themes. The backdrop is death; the text, "Eternity
is Now," whether in the embrace of a woman, or in the
exultation accompanying the retrospective vision, or in the
dying of the self in nature's "lively May." Death is more of a
Presence than in earlier poems, and the tone is more urgent.
The intensity is reflected by the verbs that change from hearing, knowing, and seeing to burning, daring, and beating as
the soul "moans to be reborn!" So painful is the process, so
frustrating the experience of losing, finding, and losing again
that the speaker almost despairs:

A slow growth is a hard thing to endure.
When figures out of obscure shadow rave,
All sensual love's but dancing on a grave.

Outstaring death, "A spirit raging at the visible," he holds on
and holds out. Finally, as Frederick Hoffman notes, he "persuades himself of death."[26] The moment conquered—"I
breathe alone until my dark is light"—he comes to terms
with the cycle of birth and death: "I think a bird, and it
begins to fly,/By dying daily, I have come to be." The final
words, with their evocation of becoming, are a prelude to the
final passage, "They Sing, They Sing." The poem is replete
with dance images—neither erotic nor dancing-mad—but the
slow, undulating movements of women dancing "in a dying
light" and the dance of light itself as it descends to darkness
and oblivion. The birds sing of Eternity much like Yeats's
golden bird, "Of what is past, or passing, or to come." The
vision that "moves, and yet remains the same" reminds the
poet of himself—"I dread the thing I am"—but he can know
the self finally. He has confronted "Death's possibilities" and
though he cannot sing, like the birds, he can register his
defiance against the terror and the void. "All experience is a
dying," Roethke once said: "The marsh, the mire, the void
are always there." The final lines of "The Dying Man" are
the only apotheosis Roethke could perceive—a still point at
the heart of all motion:

Nor can imagination do it all
In this last place of light; he dares to live
Who stops being a bird, yet beats his wings
Against the immense immeasurable emptiness of things.

"Meditations of an Old Woman," a sequence of five long
poems, is the archetypal journey of the spirit as it struggles
toward definition: "The spirit moves, but not always up-

ward." Again, the journey is interior: "The body, delighting in thresholds,/Rocks in and out of itself." The old woman merges with the image of herself in youth—dancing her escape into pure sensation. And the recollection brings the rebirth of calm itself: "Ask all the mice who caper in the straw—/I am benign in my own company./A shape without a shade, or almost none,/I hum in pure vibration, like a saw." As always in Roethke's poetry, the dance of pure motion is uplifting, beneficent if mad, "the grandeur of a crazy one alone." In the final meditation, the woman strikes a theme that will persist in the rest of Roethke's poetry: the tenacity of an unceasing pattern of movement. Here, the old woman sees herself as "beginner,/Perpetual beginner," stubbornly "longing for absolutes that never come." In loneliness, like Gerontion, terrified by "the dance of natural objects in the mind," she experiences a series of metamorphoses of the self—from lark, worm, stone, "nimble girl" to a sense of significance: "I rock in my own dark,/Thinking, God has need of me." Thus, "released from the dreary dance of opposites," the old woman's spirit soars upward: "I live in light's extreme; I stretch in all directions," finally coming to acceptance and stasis: "Yea, I have gone and stayed." The poem is a beautiful affirmation of birth, life, *and* death. Later, in "Meditation at Oyster River," Roethke will reconcile those antitheses finally:

> Now in this waning of light,
> I rock with the motion of morning.

In 1960, Roethke wrote in a letter to Ralph Mills a short verse that might serve as epigraph to his final volume, *The Far Field*.

> I would praise:
> —Those who will be compelled to dance
> Through a final flame.

The motif of necessary ritual enclosed in this final image of dancing distinguishes Roethke's last poems. His lifelong pre-occupation with death now becomes the central theme that encompasses as well the search for a "metaphysical experience." There is a coming full circle in *The Far Field* as Roethke recaptures the early spirit and fascination of the greenhouse Eden, now the microcosm for all the grown man's experiences. Privately and poetically, Roethke had been journeying backward in time, believing with characteristic optimism: "Out of these nothings/All beginnings come." Originally, the sequence of poems was to be titled, "Dance On, Dance On, Dance On," for Roethke could envision no world—here or elsewhere—where motion ceases. Man dancing back to his first innocence or forth to death in some inexorable rhythm of the cosmos was all he chose to express or perhaps understand. *The Far Field* is such a sequence with its indication of the moving pattern and its emphasis on the lone human discovering, thinking, moving, dancing, and finally journeying out of the self into oblivion. The peace and harmony that suffuse a poem like "The Rose" provide a kind of still point for the entire volume.

In *The Far Field*, Roethke's last speculations of the transitory nature of human experience, he rejects finally the escape into pure sensuality. As we know from "The Sensualists," physical pleasure unrelieved by spiritual union is insufficient. Now in "The Longing," the theme is played upon more insistently: "Lust fatigues the soul./How to transcend this sensual emptiness?" Thus the poems of the "North American Sequence" constitute a search that begins in longing, moves toward meditation, continues in Roethke's "journey to the interior" through the long waters to the far field, and closes with his emblem poem of perfect harmony: the motions of man with the stillness of the rose.

"The Longing" begins at the nadir of despair, the spirit reminiscent of the opening lines of Eliot's *Ash-Wednesday* ("Because I do not hope to turn again/Because I do not hope"), but there the ritual of losing all prefigures rebirth. Here, the poet "in a bleak time, when a week of rain is a year," finds himself in a wasted world in which motionlessness is lifelessness:

> The great trees no longer shimmer;
> Not even the soot dances.
> . . . .
> And the spirit fails to move forward,

Wallace Stevens's own *final man* suggests the stage of the speaker:

> We live in an old chaos of the sun,
> Or old dependency of day or night,
> Or island solitude, unsponsored, free,
> Of that wide water, inescapable. . . .

Here in "The Longing," man, free and alone, seeks "beginnings." The final section of the poem is the dance back to life through the now-familiar cycle of metamorphoses:

> I would with the fish, the blackening salmon, and the mad
> lemmings,
> The children dancing, the flowers widening.
> . . . .
> I long for the imperishable quiet at the heart of form.

Like the Eliot of "East Coker" he too would be an explorer. The poem introduces the central themes of the sequence: a journey to death, the solitary nature of that experience, and the mode of its occurrence—often a dance—as the poet moves from dark to light, despair to hope, death to rebirth. The images of the rose, the dance, and the journey which unite the series and prefigure the final poem are presented here. As always in Roethke's best poems, the movement is expressed in the lilting, dancing lyric carefully balanced by the sober reflective tone that accompanies his search for permanence and stillness.

"The Long Waters" evokes Eliot's *Four Quartets* with its archetypal images of elemental birth ("I return where fire has been,/To the charred edge of the sea") which become the agents of his own renascence. Again taking his model from nature ("butterflies, yellow and blue,/Rejoice in the language of smells and dancing") the poet controls his fear of the "dubious sea-change" and takes courage for the "fall." In the advancing and retreating waters of the changing sea, he envisions his own birth and death, but even more he senses a divinity in his presence:

The eternal one, the child, the swaying vine branch
The numinous ring around the opening flower,
The friend that runs before me on the windy headlands. . . .

For the first time in Roethke's poetry, there is a profound sense of *becoming* as prophetically he awaits death:

I am gathered together once more;
I embrace the world.

Finally, the experience is a private one, as the poet without lover, father, or creatures in nature loses and finds himself in the long water; he acquiesces to death.

Admittedly, reconciliations are not frequent in Roethke's experience; poems written after "The Rose" confront the terrifying abyss: "Can I outleap the sea—/The edge of all land, the final sea?"* He asks, "Do we move toward God, or merely another condition?" yet he can assert, "We come to something without knowing why." Always, the movements of the body accompany the upward surge of the will, so that

*Recalling "Someday I'll Step with Arrowed Grace."

the final poems of *The Far Field* are often illuminated with
joyous dancing.

But madness and despair are always specters to be dealt
with in Roethke's world. In "The Abyss" which follows the
poet into the hospital, into the terror and violence of mental
breakdown, he can still glimpse a moment of moving unity:

> In this, my half-rest,
> Knowing slows for a moment,
> And not-knowing enters, silent,
> Bearing being itself,
> And the fire dances
> To the stream's
> Flowing.

Recreating again the Protean changes that bring him from
the abyss into the light ("I have merged, like the bird, with
the bright air") he comes to life again and hope. But this is
not the joy of sexual abandon; "We struggled out of sensuality," he relates, and the dance in "The Tranced" is a formal-
ized ritual of worship reflecting the triumph of opposites in
nature itself:

> Our eyes fixed on a point of light so fine
> Subject and object sang and danced as one;
> Slowly we moved between
> The unseen and the seen,
> Our bodies light, and lighted by the moon.

"Sequence, Sometimes Metaphysical" is the last group of
poems in *The Far Field* and at first seems to be a regression
into that dark world of the mental hospital Roethke knew too
intimately. Roethke's critics greeted the publication of the
poems with enthusiasm. Stanley Kunitz viewed them as the
emblem of Roethke's spiritual crisis, "the dance of the soul
around the exhausted flesh and toward the divine fire."[27]

James Dickey described them as "the cries of a creature in a landscape which is beautiful and filled with mystery and does not know that it is: the utterances of a perceiving mind which cannot enter wholly into nature and yet yearns to."[28] As Mills suggests, the poems are more spare, formal, compressed, though the series recapitulates all the fear and dread, joy and celebration of earlier poems.[29] But the tone is more controlled, reflective, and tranquil than they first appear to suggest.

The opening poem, "In A Dark Time," expresses the central motif to be preserved through the sequence: "In a dark time, the eye begins to see." The "dark time" is the recurrent mental breakdown, the labored journey to self-knowledge: "A man goes far to find out what he is—/Death of the self in the long, tearless night." Teetering on the edge, he is faced with the "steady storm of correspondences!" and the attempt to survive that storm and arrive restored to peace and stillness is the matter of the poems. Thus in "The Sequel" the poet momentarily escapes into a dream in which he is engaged in a cosmic dance of celebration:

> I saw a body dancing in the wind,
> A shape called up out of my natural mind;
> I heard a bird stir in its true confine;
> A nestling sighed—I called that nestling mine;
> A partridge drummed; a minnow nudged its stone;
> We danced, we danced, under a dancing moon;
> And on the coming of the outrageous dawn,
> We danced together, we danced on and on.

The dream over, the waking man knows a momentary wellbeing, but the images of swaying and dancing give way to pacing as he returns to the world of the hospital, the imprisonment of the spirit. That the experience occurs in the *dark time*, when as poet-madman-*vates* he touches on the divine, is a familiar theme in Roethke's poetry. "Dancing-mad,"

Roethke unites himself with something pure, bright, and numinous.

"The Motion" is quite simply Roethke's final reach, though fragile and imperfect, toward God: that ultimate *dance* in Roethke's lexicon. In a quiet, musing voice, he attempts to fuse the antitheses of flesh and spirit into one upward striving movement. "The soul has many motions, body one," he observes and the erotic movement of the one conjoins in love with the complex and various "stretchings" of the other toward the single goal. In the spirit of Donne and Marvell, the poet finds in the emblem of the butterfly a correlative for his own spiritual state: wind-tattered, pulsing downward to death while lusting for life. The dramatic juxtaposition of suffering and striving is conveyed in the grieving, the torment, the damaged wings, the creaking, and the crying as contrasted to the *reaching*. The butterfly *stretches* its spirit; the poet *rises* in his mind, dares, embraces, strides. Although he reaches (in the sense of arrives at) this final solitude, he "reaches beyond his death." The irony contained in these opposed associations prepares us for the final stanza in which Roethke fuses images of hope and frailty into one cry of affirmation:

> Wings without feathers creaking in the sun,
> The closing dirt dancing on a sunless stone
> God's night and day: down this space He has smiled,
> Hope has its hush: we move through its broad day,—
> O who would take the vision from the child?—
> O, motion O, our chance is still to be!

"The Restored" is a dance of celebration as the soul rises from its defeat by reason and experiences rebirth. The fundamental opposition between the mind and the spirit is expressed in terms of a war in the arena of the soul, resolved only when the emotions take over and—like Yeats's dancing girl—outdance thought. Again, the soul is imaged in the

twin metaphor of butterfly and woman as it moves through
the cycle of life, death, and rebirth:

> And danced, at high noon,
> On a hot, dusty stone,
> In the still point of light
> Of my last midnight.

The theme of accepting without understanding is reiterated
in "The Right Thing" in which "the right thing can happen
to the right man" only when he can accept the miracle of
universal oneness without penetrating its mystery with the
mind. Thus the eternal paradox: "Child of the dark, he can
outleap the sun," is the final wisdom Roethke accedes to. In
"The Abyss" he had written "I rock between dark and dark,"
but looking back on his poetic life in the year of his untimely
death, 1963, he mused, "I count myself a happy poet." The
experiences of despair and exultation provide the cyclic process of almost every Roethke poem, but in "Once More the
Round," the last poem in *The Far Field*, the poet dances his
joy and love of life. The poem is a resolution of the vexations
of the spirit and the affirmation of a truth he had struggled a
lifetime to accept: the unity of all things in nature and in
man. Perceiving the cyclic pattern of life in Papa's greenhouse, he knows himself to be one with leaf, bird, fish, and
snail. The occasion is marked by the performance of a
round—the simple, measured dance of country people who
yearly celebrated both the return of spring to the land with
its promise of rebirth and the climax of the harvest in the
summer season of plenitude. But, as Joseph Gregor had observed, "We dance to free ourselves from the fear of life and
we dance *only* if we can set ourselves free."[30] Theodore
Roethke, in a moment of exhilarating freedom, commemo-
rates his release from reason and his surrender to the pure
ecstasy of senses:

What's greater, Pebble or Pond?
What can be known? The Unknown.
My true self runs toward a Hill
More! O More! visible.
Now I adore my life
With the Bird, the abiding Leaf,
With the Fish, the questing Snail,
And the Eye altering all;
And I dance with William Blake
For love, for Love's sake;

And everything come to One,
As we dance on, dance on, dance on.

To *see* "thro' the eye" is Blake's text; and the poet dances with Blake with whom he shares the divine poetic gift, "To see the world in a grain of sand." Blake had proclaimed, "If the doors of perception were cleansed, everything would appear to man as it is, infinite." The final lines of "Once More the Round" are Roethke's perception of eternity—a dance of cosmic proportions spiraling infinitely. It has no beginning or end as we know it, but like the cyclical process of birth, death, and rebirth its motions are steadfast and insistent. It is a dance we can feel in the beat of the blood: "I hear my being dance from ear to ear." Now, tuned in to that internal rhythm, he could accept his dissolution into the inexorable cycle of the universe. In "The Stony Garden" Roethke had written that the isolation each man is heir to breaks down when he hears "two songs, one outward, one inward/Echoing on each side of the glass."[31]

Early in his quest for the self, Roethke wrote,

Who lives at the dark center
Has his own brightness,
An aura of flame beyond being,
But no answer

134

In "Once More the Round" he is ready, finally, to accept the vision of a universal oneness that includes all dancers and himself. Dante's conviction, fortified by his first glimpse of Paradise—"La Gloria di colui che tutto move/per l'universo penetra" (The Glory of He who moves all things penetrates the universe)—becomes Roethke's own belief, sensed in the greenhouse and tested in the arena of his inner being. "Dancing his way out of his body toward God,"[32] as Spender envisioned him, Theodore Roethke was his own "one-legged man," invoking God to make him less clumsy, reaching toward grace and harmony and stillness:

> Sing all beginnings, sing,
> Dance, dance, one-legged man.
> . . . .
> It's time that we begin. . . .

Modern poets don't speak too much of heaven: for T. S. Eliot the purgatorial struggle was sufficiently ennobling; for Wallace Stevens the changing beauty of the earthly paradise was sufficiently enduring. For Theodore Roethke, who saw all experience as "a dying,"[33] heaven was some indeterminate place where "True dancers shall foregather."[34] The triumph over time and space, as the philosopher Ernst Cassirer tells us in his observation of mythic man, comes when he finds in his own consciousness the threads that link him to the past and he achieves universal harmony by dissolving into the collective unconscious. Thus his security rests in knowing he is part of its indivisibility. Such is the function of the dance in all of Roethke's poetry from the beginning to "Once More the Round"—to consummate, validate, and celebrate his union with all living things both visible and invisible.

NOTES

1. Letter to Allan Seager, 8 May 1943, in Roethke, *Selected Letters*, ed. Mills, 1968, p. 109.

2. Letter to Allan Seager, 13 Sept. 1953, in Roethke, *Letters*, p. 110.

3. Graham, *The Dance in America*, 1976.

4. Ibid.

5. Letter to Babette Deutsch, 22 January 1948, in Roethke, *Letters*, p. 140.

6. Mary Wigman, *The Language of Dance* (Middletown, Conn.: Wesleyan University Press, 1963), p. 110.

7. Ibid., p. 41.

8. Graham.

9. Stephen Spender, "The Objective Ego," in *Theodore Roethke*, ed. Arnold Stein (Seattle: University of Washington Press, 1965), p. 3.

10. Letter to Babette Deutsch, 22 January 1948, in Roethke, *Letters*, p. 142.

11. Notebook 35, no. 61, in *On the Poet and His Craft: Selected Prose of Theodore Roethke*, ed. Ralph J. Mills, Jr. (Seattle: University of Washington Press, 1965), p. 61.

12. Ernst Cassirer, *The Philosophy of Symbolic Forms*, vol. II: *Mythical Thought* (New Haven: Yale University Press, 1955), p. 39.

13. Stanley Kunitz, "Theodore Roethke," *New York Review of Books*, 17 October 1963, pp. 21–22.

14. Blessing, *Theodore Roethke's Dynamic Vision*, 1974, p. 5.

15. Spender, p. 5.

16. Seager, *The Glass House*, p. 56.

17. "In A Dark Time," TV program, ed. David Myers, 1963.

18. Seager, p. 75.

19. Heilman, "Theodore Roethke: Personal Notes," 1964, pp. 55–56.

20. Spender, p. 5.

21. Published in *American Poetry Journal*, November 1934. Later title changed to "Someday I'll Step"; published in Roethke *Letters*, as "More Pure Than Flight," pp. 23–24.

22. Letter to Kenneth Burke, 5 November 1952, Roethke, *Letters*, p. 181.

23. Letter to Peter Viereck, 21 June 1953, ibid., p. 191.

24. Letter to Arabel Porter, 1 May 1953, ibid., p. 186.

25. Blessing, p. 173.

26. Frederick J. Hoffman, "Theodore Roethke: The Poetic Shape of Death," in Stein, p. 108.

27. Kunitz, "Poet of Transformations," 1965, p. 25.

28. James Dickey, *Review of Sequence, Sometimes Metaphysical* in *Poetry*, November 1964, p. 121.

29. Ralph J. Mills, Jr., "In the Way of Becoming: Roethke's Last Poems," in Stein, p. 116.

30. Joseph Gregor, "Panorchesis," in *The Dance Has Many Faces*, ed. Sorell, 1951.

31. In Roethke, *Straws from the Fire*, ed. Wagoner, 1972, pp. 50–51.

32. Spender, p. 5.

33. "In A Dark Time."

34. Roethke, *Straws from the Fire*, p. 223.

CHAPTER V

A Choice Among the Measures . . . :
William Carlos Williams

(Look, Dad, I'm Dancing!)
—*Paterson*

"A fine trickle of words . . . "
—"Improvisations"

"Isadora, when I saw you dance the interrupting years fell
back," William Carlos Williams wrote in 1909 in a small
verse of tribute to the radiant Isadora Duncan who had swept
the imagination of all Europe.[1] Throughout his life, Williams
would reflect his own hypnotic absorption with the dance.
All moving things respond to their own internal rhythm: the
eddying Passaic, the rumbling locomotive, the thrashing
trees, the leaping falls, "events dancing two/and two with
language," the poet "rolling up out of the chaos/a nine
months' wonder, the city/the man, an identity." And all dynamic motion is a dance: "The measure intervenes, to measure is all we know,/a choice among the measures/the measured dance." As we examine Williams's poetry and prose,
dance appears to be a significant term in his lexicon; its
dynamic force creates the Third World the poem stakes out;
"otherwise it would all die voiceless." More than any other
poet in the twentieth century, Williams fuses the gesture and
the word: "The dance! The verb detaches itself/Seeking to
become articulate."

139

"To make a start" in the poetry of William Carlos Williams is of necessity to *name*. "The only means the artist has to give value to life is to recognize it with the imagination and name it," he wrote in *Spring and All*. So it is that any understanding of his art must begin with the word, for Williams's worlds come into being, like the Creation itself, with the ritual of naming. "No ideas but in things," is Williams's text, and the great body of his poetry rests upon the numinous activity of uniting the word with the unique thing as it comes into his vision. The tragic condition that assaults him everywhere in *Paterson* is that

> The language, the language
> Fails them
> They do not know the words

Providing the paradigm for an approach to his poetry, Williams invites us into what first appears to be twin worlds of his experience, only to have us discover for ourselves a mythic third. The words *are Paterson*. The rhythms begin with the recurrent words: *Invention, Imagination*, the roaring *Falls, Beautiful Thing*, the *filthy Passaic*, the *Dance*, the *Poem*—at first in no discernible pattern. Then we perceive a duality, a two-ness that Williams himself appeared to symbolize throughout his long career—the poetry and the prose of it. He was the nocturnal poet and Dr. Williams; the genial friend of artists Charles Demuth and Marcel Duchamp, of poets Kenneth Burke, Marianne Moore, Louis Zukofsky, and Ezra Pound, yet the privately intense, disappointed man tasting the bitterness of Eliot's successes; the restless escapist driving his car away from the sordid urban Jersey sprawl and the courageous Paterson leaping into the filthy Passaic. Most important, he dwelled in both the quotidian reality of Rutherford and the "other" realm of the imagination:

> So that we experience
> violently
> every day
> two worlds
> one of which we share with the
> rose in bloom
> and one,
> by far the greater
> with the past,
> the world of memory,
> the silly world of history,
> the world of the imagination.

And the sometimes violent yoking of those polar worlds brings about their coexistence in the *third* world: Art—the Poem—where each "particular" retains an integrity of its own, yet through Invention can "startle us anew."

> So through art alone, male and female, a
> field of flowers, a tapestry, spring flowers
> unequaled in loveliness.

This, the third world, the "primal meeting ground where the 'actual' and the 'imaginative' existed simultaneously."[2]

No study of dance imagery in Williams's poetry is possible without an examination of that third world as his poetry expresses it. It is delineated through a mythic perspective, but Williams's myth is something newly minted and must be comprehended on his terms.

As we review the contents of the mythic perspective recognized by philosophers and mythographers discussed in Chapter I, the comparison and contrast with Williams's third world are compelling. Only then can we say that his vision is mythic. The mere presence in *Paterson* of the stuff of the myth—the archetypal journey, the colossal giants, the recurrent patterns of death and rebirth—has suggested to some critics a total symbolic interpretation of the American experience, but—like many half-truths—this only serves to deform the poem and fly in the face of Dr. Williams's own injunction: "What I put down of value will have this value: an escape from crude symbolism, the annihilation of strained associations." Myth, in its truest sense, is a dynamic of sensuous forms. As Williams reminds us, "The word must be put down for itself, not as the symbol or nature but a part, cognizant of the whole—aware—civilized." Thus, while the metaphor "a man in himself is a city" invites us to extend the *figura*, the palpable reality of both man and city in all of their unique parts is always before us.

Ernst Cassirer observed that the mythic perspective is governed by a Universal Principle: the assumption that the *sacred* world is unified, ordered, indivisible, and self-contained. By accenting all objects and events in the world as *sacred* or *profane*, myth creates a fundamental tension that permeates all its thinking. In essence, myth *rejects* the profane in favor of a world that is transcendent, eternal, and unchanging. "All the contents of the mythical consciousness are rejoined into a whole. They form a self-enclosed realm and possess a common tonality, by which they are distinguished from the common, everyday, empirical existence."[3] Similarly, the sacred accenting affects the views of Time, Space, Number, and the cycles of life in nature and in man.

For William Carlos Williams, however, "here is everywhere." The mythical absolute of sacred or profane is impossible for Williams for whom there is no "other world" in any doctrinal sense to go to; moreover, he refuses to reject the real world—deformed and sullied as it is. As Hillis Miller points out, there is no reference to a world beyond a world.[4] Instead, Williams's world, "no ideas but in Things"—to Miller a wedding of the mind and the universe—is all-inclusive. What Williams calls his two worlds conjoin with "words" in a troika whose contiguousness, unity, and wholeness rest in the synthesizing triumph of art. Williams's third world, and the one true reality, is the Poem: "A work of art is important only as evidence, in its structure, of a new world which it has created to affirm. . . . A life that is here and now is timeless. That is the universal I am seeking: to embody that in a work of art, a new world that is always 'real.' "

Allowing for this initial distinction, we are immediately struck with the similarities between the mythic reality and Williams's third world. At times, Williams "accents" the *things* of that world, as Rexroth notes,[5] with an immanence and transcendence—the "radiant gist." He transmutes the "ordinary" with wholeness and harmony; but more often it is present in its very deformity, ugliness, and pain. There is a primal sensuousness in both the things that pass into his vision "armless, legless,/headless, packed like the pit of a fruit into/ that obscure corner" and the words he selects to recreate them as "the verb detaches itself/seeking to become articulate." A critical quality of mythic thought is the blurring of the fixed boundary between the "real" and "ideal." Thus the image that results from mythic accenting *is* the thing; it does not represent the thing. Mythical thinking contemplates only one level of reality; its consciousness resides in the immediate impression, which is absolute—not to be measured by something else. It is bound inextricably to the *concrete* and everything is viewed in biological or physical terms. Myth's predilection for the concrete is expressed in Williams's sharp sensory awareness, his tendency to communicate the organic quality of words themselves. The message of the "Red Wheelbarrow" is that "so much depends" on our possession of it through a similar awareness.

The mythic intuitions of space and time underlie much of the form of Williams's poetry. In myth, no sharp boundaries divide the world spatially: all substance shares a common spatial order. In each part of reality the structure, the form, of the whole is replicated. No detached, abstract form of space exists, and conventional spatial distinctions disappear. Similarly, in Williams's poetry, the "mind is dispersed everywhere in things and forms one with them,"[6] recalling Xenophanes' observation that "The All is One." The mind overlaps with the things and things overlap with the mind, as Miller notes. In essence, all *things* exist side by side in art, retaining their unique character while reacting to the others. Coexisting in space and time, the universal can be found in the particular and the particular in the universal, as Williams announces at the beginning of *Paterson*, and prose can "exist" in the poem with poetry, as well as history, letters, and documents. As Miller defines "spatialization" in Williams's poetry, "Each thing touches the other, interacting with the other, quarreling, rebounding, and yet keeping its definite edges and form. Each fills space, permeates it, but remains itself, uncontaminated by the others . . . everything the poet has experienced is present together." Williams establishes "places of simultaneity" where and when everything coexists as separate entities. The wheelbarrow that occupies a small space is everywhere, contains everything. Thus, as in all mythic thinking, spatial barriers dissolve.

Williams's view of time corresponds as well to mythic time, whose hallowed moment is the time of "beginning" which all rituals of rebirth reenact. Since the true character of myth is concerned with "origins," the how and why of things before history, distinctions of past, present, and future disappear and all time is a flowing together, like the river itself. In *Paterson*, especially, we are conscious of the past-in-the-present—the bits of history which revive the moment of the city's "beginnings." In fact, the words *beginning, renew, birth, new world* have a quality of purity, of ineffability, in all of Williams's poetry: "For the beginning is assuredly/the end—." The final book of *Paterson* plays on this motif as " 'the river has returned to its beginnings'/and backward/(and forward)." Thus it was natural for William to take up the theme of the "ruined garden" in *In th*

American Grain and to share Columbus's fears for the virgin land. The violation of the first Eden—time and place of origins—is, as we know, a familiar archetypal myth. Related to this theme of birth and fruition is the motif of fecundity as it reappears throughout Williams's work. His interest in the myth of Kora-Persephone and his emphasis on sensuality and birth (a natural extension of his experience as a doctor who brought, by his own count, over 2,000 babies into the world!) is revealed in multiple images relating to the "female principle." This equation of all activity with the biological in myth is articulated in Williams's prose and poetry whether in the discoveries of a new land, the "birth" of a work of art, or the wholesome love between man and woman. Reed Whittemore observes, "Each particular hero had his own particular earth to quest for but the nature of the quest is always the same. Always the earth discovered and explored was female, with the consequence the history of the Nuevo Mundo became throughout . . . a history of man chasing woman."[7] "To get at the primalcy with a whirl of words" Williams focuses on the "he and she of it." The union of male and female in myth, as in Williams's poetry, is the union of mind and fact— the Beautiful Thing of *Paterson*.

It is not possible here to detail the particularities of the mythic perspective as they appear in *Paterson*, but a study of the five parts of the poem reveals the familiar motifs of myth. We have already noted the aspects of space and time as well as the "voyage": "Rigor of beauty is the quest," defined by Whittemore as a search "for the natural order, an order implicit in the mind of Paterson and in the environment of Paterson."[8]

The "magic" of number and naming, the persona-as-prophet, and ritual all have special significance in *Paterson* and, indeed, in the majority of Williams's works. Number magic inheres in Williams's predilection for "threes"—the three worlds of Things, the Imagination, and Art; the three elements, Miller observes,[9] of Williams's "drama": "the form-

less ground, the formed thing, and the nameless presence"
(the "Beautiful Thing"); the mutual existence, noted by
Guimond,[10] of the natural, the quotidian, and the intellectual
each with a language of its own; the "line" of Williams's
major later poetry, including *Paterson*, the triadic form.

It would be difficult to overemphasize the importance of
language both to mythical thought and to William Carlos
Williams. Cassirer discusses this aspect of myth at length in
his several studies of language and myth, articulating it most
succinctly here:

> This inability of mythical thinking to apprehend pure ideal
> signification, is strikingly revealed by its relation to lan-
> guage. Myth and language are inseparable and mutually
> condition each other. Word and name magic are, like image
> magic, an integral part of the magical world view. But in all
> this the basic presupposition is that word and name do not
> merely have a function of describing or portraying but con-
> tain within them the object and its real powers. Word and
> name do not . . . signify, they are and act. In the mere sensu-
> ous matter of language, in the mere sound of the human
> voice, there resides a peculiar power over things.[11]

Thus Williams's poem is "a small machine made out of
words . . . it lives with an intrinsic movement of its own to
verify its authenticity." And Williams speaks of the poet as

> a man
> whose words will
>   bite
>   their way
> home—being actual
> having the form
> of motion

It takes the unique power of words "to give created forms
reality, actual existence," and he asserts that through the

energizing imagination, sweeping over the *things* of the world, the words *create* anew the intrinsic, yet often unreachable, order in nature: "But how will you find beauty when it is locked in the mind past all remonstrance?" The answer in *Paterson* comes in the harvest of words through which the immanent thing, the radiant gist, is revealed. "To refine, to clarify, to intensify that eternal moment in which we alone live there is a single force—the imagination." The terms of this process contain the very language of myth: rebirth, clarity, wholeness; and the artist is the "god" of myth: the omnipresent, all-seeing creator:

"The artist addresses himself to life as a whole."

"He is the whole man, not the breaker-up but the compacter."

So it is that the quester, the ubiquitous Paterson, is a kind of Tiresias who "sees all," oracular, as Gerber observes,[12] who brings back the "news," the immanent truth but with a difference. He is *also* Paterson, the fallible human being—often bewildered, directionless, fearful, indifferent, yet always searching, as the artist always must, to validate the reality he knows exists in the nature of things. In "A Study of the Artist" Williams brings together the artist, the imagination, and the eternal third world of art:

He is a man to be judged, to live or die, like other men by what he does . . . the real purpose, to lift the world of the senses to the level of the imagination and so give it new currency. . . . The imagination is the transmuter. It is the changer. Without imagination life cannot go on, for we are left staring at empty casings where truth lived yesterday while the creature itself has escaped behind us. . . . It is the power of mutation which the mind possesses to rediscover the truth. So that the artist is dealing with actualities not with dreams. . . . Think of the world of art—the poem—as a structure . . . [the poet] discovers and builds anew.

Williams reiterates this conviction throughout his career: "On the poet devolves the most vital function of society: to recreate it . . . in a new mode." Most memorably, we recall it in "Asphodel, That Greeny Flower" where the poem is the only apotheosis we can experience:

> It is difficult
> to get the news from poems
> yet men die miserably every day
> for lack
> of what is found there.

The last, and, for our purpose, most significant aspect of myth—the role of ritual—has already been dealt with in some detail in Chapter I. The importance of mythic rituals in the poetry of William Carlos Williams has never been thoroughly penetrated. If we recall that many rites are "a reactualization, through song and dance, of the essential mythical events that have taken place since the Creation," as Mircea Eliade notes,[13] in order to recapture the event and thereby "create the World anew," we can begin to appreciate Williams's use of ritual. For primitive man, rites enabled him to abolish time, celebrate his origins, exorcize his demons, mark the stages of human development through initiation, and affirm his place in the cosmos. Eliade has stressed especially the ritual of renewal in the cycle of death and rebirth in *The Myth of the Eternal Return*—a myth that underlies *Paterson* and other poems. That mythic pattern is expressed by Williams in a search for a new poetry, a new language, above all, a renewed perception of the world before him. Whether in the rite of *immersion*, the rite of *purgation* by fire, the demonic journey of *Kora in Hell* ("giants in the dirt"), or the descent and ascent of *Paterson*, the central ritual in Williams's work is one of death and rebirth in endless cycles. There are other rituals in his poetry, notably the dance which conveys a multiplicity of experiences—often containing these mythic patterns. As we shall see, Williams's dance, like many primitive rituals, is frequently a celebration. Despite the broken world he enters—and we recall Hart Crane's words most vividly: "And so it was I entered the broken world . . . my word I poured"—Williams's poetry is from the beginning to the end a celebration of life, as he captures it in "isolate flecks."

The aim of myth is to fix man's place in the universe, to assure his survival through the cyclic pattern of birth/death/rebirth, and thus to allow him to measure himself as part of an enduring reality. Williams's poetry as well strives toward such realization, but such redemptive experiences come "in that eternal moment in which we alone live" rather than in the permanent beauty of a distant Paradise. Williams's mythic world "leaps from a varnish pot" and becomes "intertwined with fire," becoming that "Beautiful Thing" whose "vulgarity of beauty surpassed all . . . perfections."

So it is that the dance in Williams's poetry and prose must be viewed against the backdrop of the sordid, tragic, yet always retrievable world. "All men by their nature praise," he wrote, and in his most moving declaration of faith, he affirms that even the plain, the green and wooden asphodel "celebrates the light." Williams's dance is always touched with the ineffable quality of the poem itself: "The words of the thing twang and twitter to the gentle rocking of a high-laced boot and the silk above that. The trick of the dance is in following now the words. . . . "

Whether on the plane of the imagination, or in the ceaseless motions of the natural world, or in his own "kinesthetic pantomime,"[14] Williams's dance is a recurrent image, crucial to our understanding of *his* vision of the world. He loved to dance, admitting—like Roethke—his own gracelessness. "Dancing is all the exercise my legs need," he wrote home while studying medicine at the University of Pennsylvania. Together with Ezra Pound and H. D. he "had a great time singing and dancing."[15] Even before he met Lincoln Kirstein

(1932) or wrote Kay Boyle (1922): "A poet should take his inspiration from the other arts. . . . Maybe there is something running through . . . the Dance?" he knew the art of Angna Enters and had reported his enjoyment of the ballet in Paris. His dance is always touched with a luminousness that elevates the shabbiest carnival—in Spain where the girls do the fandango in the streets—and in Santo Domingo where the pitiful prostitutes perform in the burlesques. He creates for all time the image of himself as satyr in "Danse Russe": "I in my north room/dance naked, grotesquely/before my mirror," and in 1915 he would trace, as the cover design for *Al Que Quiere!*, the markings on a pebble which "looked like a dancer . . . a natural, completely individual pattern."[16] After his death in 1963, a fragment for a sixth part of *Paterson* still evokes that lifelong passion: "Dance, dance! loosen your limbs from that art which holds you/faster than the drugs which hold you faster—dandelion on/my bedroom wall."

On a primary level, the dance in Williams's poetry and prose is the catharsis of emotions as natural to man as singing, lovemaking, laughing, or weeping. Compelled by his being to "Dance! Sing! Coil and Uncoil!" man translates his misery, brokenness, and anguish into the language of gestures. Thus the tarantella records the intensity, the primitive feeling, the deep sensuality that "leaves the mind in tatters." Men must dance to that inexorable music, he writes in *Kora in Hell*, confessing, "but for broken feet beating, beating on worn flagstones, I would have danced to my knees at the fiddler's first run." The darkies "dancing in Mayaguez" weave away, beat back their agony and pangs of loneliness. Dance is their sublimation. Invoking the hidden musicians, the poet in *Kora* joins his natural motions with those of the world around him: "—and I? I must dance with the wind, make my own snowflakes, whistle a contrapuntal melody to my own fugue! Huzza then, this is the dance of the blue moss bank! Huzza then, this is the mazurka of the hollow log! Huzza then, this is the dance of rain in the cold trees!" The intimation here and elsewhere is one of harmonizing, unifying rhythm in the dance itself that makes the fusion of these opposites a viable possibility.

Behind all of Williams's references to the dance lie the assumptions of myth. As dance was the ritualized activity returning the shaman to the time of beginnings, identifying him with the gods through his repetition of paradigmatic gestures, uniting him with the universal rhythms of the cosmos, and celebrating his identity with eternal and immutable things—so Williams's dance often generates harmony, balance, oneness. Translating his symbiotic worlds into the third world of art, Williams's dance incarnates that union. "Out of bitterness itself the clear wine of the imagination will be pressed and the dance prosper thereby." While at times his dance is the primitive, sexual, orgiastic motions of the pagan gods "that danced beside Helicon" (the "giants in the dirt" who "dance as much as they ever did") it is also that beneficent shared ritual which brings within its compass "all things and ages" met in fellowship. No need, Williams tells us, to believe in god or hell—only "the dance: hands touching, leaves touching—eyes looking, clouds rising—lips touching, cheeks touching, arm about. . . . " Human relationships, man's relationship with nature, ideas and things—all communicate through the dance.

The image of the dance relates as well, in Williams's poetry, to his perception of the imagination of the artist. He had written in *Kora*, "A thing known passes out of the mind into the muscles." Always suspicious of abstraction, repudiating the sterility of the mind *removed* from concrete reality, Williams thinks with his body. Since the dance recreates a life-giving force, patterns itself into art, and harmonizes the disparate fragments of existence into a coherent whole, it would provide Williams with a fitting metaphor for the imaginative faculty of art. Kenneth Burke, in his discussion of "symbolic action,"[17] summons up the dance of the mind involving the whole body as the essence of the poetic process. The correlation between mind and body—the conviction that poets "dance a state of mind"—is clearly manifested in Williams's definition of the imagination. In a simple transposition, the creating imagination becomes a dance in all Williams's poetry and prose. Like the sparrow who "loves to/flutter his wings/ in the dust—" the poet dances his experience into art.

Depending on Williams's mood, his dance at times summons up Shelley's singing skylark whose "unpremeditated art" celebrates life; at times, it is the consummate craftsmanship that balances with studied yet delicate gestures the antitheses inherent in those polar worlds of mind and objects. Williams's explanation of his poetic technique, the variable foot, bears out his concern with form and freedom, spontaneity and control—the tension of opposites intrinsic to modern dance. The triadic measure of Williams's later poetry, a fine balance of form and variation, permitted the patterned rhythms for the dance as well as freedom for the play of the imagination—the almost infinite modulation, as Guimond has noted.[18]

The poem, therefore, is Williams's ultimate dance. All art conforms to a single order, *measuring* out of chaos and discordance patterns of composition and coherence: "All is confusion, yet it comes from a hidden desire for the dance, a lust of the imagination, a will to accord two instruments in a duet." Thus the "poem's attenuated power which draws perhaps many broken things into a dance giving them . . . a full being." Williams warns us not to wish for floating visions of "unknown purport" but to observe "the imaginative qualities of the actual things being perceived" as they "accompany their gross vision in a slow dance, interpreting as they go." As the imagination, evoking rhythm, pattern, beauty, and joyousness, compels *everything* to movement—so poet and listener, once "the language is set down as heard," are "left free to mingle in the dance." As Williams said:

> One may write music and music but who will dance to it?

It's tunes bring the world dancing to your house-door, even on this swampside.

One must dance as he can, Williams affirms, and as the poet upon whom "devolves the most vital function of society: to recreate it," he will "set the world working or dancing again." In that third world where ideas and things coexist simultaneously, where the particular *is* the universal, all things dance.

> Rise from the ground to dance
> with joyous tread

The Poems

Williams's "poetic" reading of American history, *In the American Grain*, recreates the infamous event of the Maypole of Merry Mount by combining a series of accounts of that Bacchanalian festivity on May Day 1627. Prefigured by the description of the young Pocahontas's pagan dancing (in Strachey's *Historie**):

> ... a well-figured, but wanton yong girle, Powhatan's daughter, sometymes resorting to our fort, of the age of eleven or twelve years, get the boyes forth with her into the market place, and make them wheele, falling on their hands, turning up their heels upwards, whome she would followe, and wheele so herself, naked as she was,

the "gambol on the green" at Merry Mount is presented as both a solemn revel and a mad orgy. Bradford's account, clearly prophetic of the furious retaliation by the Puritan fathers, both fascinated and amused Williams:

> They also set up a May-pole, drinking and dancing about it many days together, inviting the Indian women, for their

*See Hart Crane's use of Strachey's account in Chapter III.

consorts, dancing and frisking together (like so many fairies, or furies rather) and worse practices. As if they had anew revived and celebrated ... practieses of the madd Bacchinalians. Morton likewise (to shew his poetrie) composed sundry rimes and verses, some tending to lascivi-ousnes, and others to the detraction and scandall of some persons, which he affixed to this idle or idoll Maypolle.

Understandably, the Puritan response enraged and horrified Williams; they had "countered with violence." He indicts their perversion, malice, envy, and insanity. "The May-Pole of Merry Mount" reflects Williams's perennial interest in dance rituals and his sympathy for "the harmless mirth of younge men." So, too, many of his early titles—"Rumba! Rumba!" "The Dance of the Locomotive," "Ballet," "Danse Russe," and "The Dance"—suggest the introduction of dance images in his poetry that would reach fullest expression in *Paterson* and *Pictures from Brueghel.*

The dance in Williams's earlier, shorter poems conjures up images of sensual, erotic, ritualized celebration not unlike the wanton merriment of 1627. The union with a life force in nature, in classical myth, in woman, in the hidden self through dancing becomes the climactic activity; the possibil-ity for artistic expression through a dynamic imagination is touched upon inchoately.

"Postlude"—a song to awaken the cooled passions—in-vokes those pagan deities worshiping at the temple of Isis to arm the lovers against the hostile stars that "swarm to de-stroy" them: "Give me hand for the dances,/Ripples at Philae, in and out. . . . " In "Canthara" two dances are juxta-posed that elicit, in their spontaneity and sensuality, the orgi-astic celebration of the body: one beautiful, the other "satyri-cally" obscene!

> The old black-man showed me
> how he had been shocked

in his youth
by six women, dancing
a set-dance, stark naked below
the skirts raised round
their breasts:
    Bellies flung forward
knees flying!
        —while
his gestures, against the
tiled wall of the dingy bath-room,
swished with ecstasy to
the familiar music of
    his old emotion.

The theme of the dancing satyr figures early in Williams's
poetry and reappears in *Paterson*. He had written in *Kora*:

I should write a happy poem tonight. It would have to do
with a bare, upstanding fellow whose thighs bulge with a
zest for—say, a zest! He tries his arm. Flings a stone over
the river. Scratches his bare back. Twirls his beard, laughs
softly and stretches up his arm in a yawn.—stops in the
midst—looking! . . . The poet transforms himself into a
satyr and goes in pursuit of a white skinned dryad. . . .

The vision would culminate in "Danse Russe," that primitive, Dionysian rite of well-being.

If when my wife is sleeping
and the baby and Kathleen
are sleeping
and the sun is a flame-white disc
in silken mists
above shining trees,—
if I in my north room
dance naked, grotesquely
before my mirror

155

waving my shirt round my head
and singing softly to myself:
"I am lonely, lonely.
I was born to be lonely,
I am best so!"
If I admire my arms, my face,
my shoulders, flanks, buttocks
against the yellow drawn shades,—

Who shall say I am not
the happy genius of my household?

The title of the poem, a gloss on the Ballet Russe whose chill, perfected beauty was too much removed from the real world to satisfy Williams, suggests a dance perhaps less graceful but more spontaneous, sensual, human and no less beautiful. There is a pattern in "Danse Russe" implicit in the rhythms of the poem, in the anapests, assonance, and alliteration, which creates dance itself. Unlike the illusory spectacle at the Metropolitan Opera House, his dance is self-expression, inner-directed—for no audience but himself. Celebrating his loneliness, the "happy genius" encompasses the reality that lies beyond the silken mists and the shining trees. Called to his dance by Pan's "sweet pipe," as he would write later in "Two Pendants for the Ears," each of us rises "from the ground to dance/with joyous tread," sensing the self in the bone and muscle and dancing that discovery in endless rites. The solitary dancer is sometimes the young lover of "Keller Gegen Dom" who "whirls himself/ obediently to/the curl of the hill/some wind-dancing afternoon," even as the stars dance their defiance of the midnight darkness; and sometimes he is the young doctor of "January Morning," alone on the Weehawken ferry, who whirls himself in abandon as he celebrates awakening in the dead season. All burgeoning things sustain his joy—he comes alive in this "beginning" time, the January morning. The doctor's dance is adumbrated in the rush of movement around him as the sun dips, the shadows drop, the horse shakes its head, the fire burns, the car rails gleam, the waves move. First water and sky converge in *him*, then winter and summer:

> The young doctor is dancing with happiness
> in the sparkling wind, alone
> at the prow of the ferry! He notices
> the curdy barnacles and broken ice crusts
> left at the slip's base by the low tide
> and thinks of summer and green
> shell-crusted ledges among
> > the emerald eel-grass!

And as he dances, the poem takes shape in the mind. Addressing his grandmother, the poet declares:

> All this—
> > was for you, old woman.
> I wanted to write a poem
> that you would understand.

The elements in "January Morning" will become familiar in Williams's poetry: the season of winter (death, age, enervation); then hints of life waiting breathlessly to be born as things begin to move and flow imperceptibly at first; then the stirring of the imagination and its dance bringing things and ideas into unison; and finally the birth of the poem that needed to be written. The theme of "January Morning" is one Williams would recreate in "Spring and All" where amidst the "waste of broad, muddy fields/brown with dried weeds" new life pushes through: "One by one objects are defined—/It quickens: clarity, outline of leaf/But now the stark dignity of/entrance—Still, the profound change/has come upon them: rooted, they/grip down and begin to awaken."

In "The Unison" the fusion of life and death in the accompanying dance revives again the rituals that mark the cyclic stages in man and nature. Here, all dance "in unison": the living with the dead, young and old, stones and brookwater, beginning and end; and though "there it is/and we can't shift it or change/it or parse it or alter it/in any way," we commemorate the pattern in a ritual that celebrates the cycle of life in all things:

> a shrine cinctured there by
> the trees, a certainty of music!
> a unison and a dance, joined
> at this death's festival: Something
> of a shed snake's skin, the beginning
> goldenrod.

At the end of the poem, we are urged to "Hear the unison of their voices" and at the grave's edge, we know "the great sun will rise—" and the cycle renew itself.

In "Romance Moderne" a modern ballet with its surrealistic images of white and green perceived through the rain-driven windshield of the poet's car, the stream's rising, falling, turning, drawing, churning, and plunging are followed by the dance of the trees and then to the poet's "other" dance:

> Trees vanish-reappear-vanish:
> detached dance of gnomes—as a talk
> dodging remarks, glows and fades.
> —The unseen power of the words—
> And now that a few of the moves
> are clear the first desire is
> to fling oneself out at the side into
> the other dance, to other music.

Peer Gynt. Rip Van Winkle. Diana.
If I were young I would try a new alignment—

158

alight nimbly from the car, Goodbye!—
Childhood companions linked two and two
criss-cross: four, three, two, one.
Back into the self, tentacles withdrawn.

Here as elsewhere in Williams's dance, the motions suggest
an awakening: Rip's coming back from the dream to the
reality beyond the windshield to the "other dance, to other
music"—the third world in which fantasy and fact coexist,
then finally "back into self," where all renewal must take
place. The theme of nature's birth and growth as a dance
reappears in "Winter Quiet"—the stasis of the year when the
life beneath the bleached grass waits for its release:

> Limb to limb, mouth to mouth
> with the bleached grass
> silver mist lies upon the back yards
> among the outhouses.
> > The dwarf trees
> pirouette awkwardly to it—
> whirling round on one toe;
> the big tree smiles and glances
> > upward!
> Tense with suppressed excitement
> the fences watch where the ground
> has humped an aching shoulder for
> > the ecstasy.

The persistence of the dwarf trees' dance to the silver mist,
despite the apparent deadness of the winter quiet and the
backdrop of the outhouses (man's violation of the essential
cleanness of nature), contributes to the poem's "suppressed
excitement" as well, reinforced by the smile, the glance upward, and the ecstasy. The response of the dwarf trees corresponds to the dancer in "The Girl," idly observed by the poet
"walking difficultly" over sand and stones. Surmounting the

sea wall, triumphantly, "She stood up dusted off her skirt/ then there lifted her feet/unencumbered to skip dancing away." Once again the dance is the joyful celebration that conquering danger and difficulty initiates. The crucial words here are "unencumbered" and "dancing" as girl and observer taste her freedom. Except for the biting sarcasm of "Lust- spiel" in which, after the guns and death, "Vienna the Volk iss very lustig,/she makes no sorry for anything!/She likes to dance and sing!" the dance in Williams's early poetry is nat- ural to man and nature, beneficent in its power to harmonize and uplift. The dance is the *activity* of union and the union itself, the wanton, free gestures transformed by the dancing rhythms of the words. And the potentiality of the dance, hidden yet present in the prosaic world we live in, is, like the poem waiting to be "discovered," waiting to be recognized: the "radiant gist" in the pitchblende.

The "Overture to a Dance of the Locomotive" was read by Williams at the Armory Show in 1913 and both recalls Whitman's own power to glimpse beauty in the mechanized world and anticipates Hart Crane's "Proem" to *The Bridge*. The poem is alive with the movement of the rumbling train: the "rubbing feet/of those coming to be carried quicken a/ grey pavement into soft light that rocks/to and fro"; the hands of the clock seem to dance; the porters "run on narrow platforms." The last part of the poem keeps a measured beat with the turning wheels: "In time: twofour!/In time: two- eight." In the final lines, the poet observes the harmony of opposites:

> wheels repeating
> the same gesture remain relatively
> stationary: rails forever parallel
> return on themselves infinitely.
> > The dance is sure.

The "certainty of music" Williams had noted in "A Unison," here the sureness of the dance in the infinite cycle of beginnings and ends, would be reaffirmed again and again in *Paterson*. In "The Lesson" he would observe that the hydrangea's "thought lies communal with the brooding worm"; it is the air whose "wanton dancing" permits it to live or die. But in "The Dance," a later poem in *Pictures from Brueghel*, Williams will take us a step further:

> But only the dance is sure!
> make it your own.
> Who can tell
> what is to come of it?

We too are like the hydrangeas as

> this flurry of a storm
> that holds us,
> plays with us and discards us
> dancing, dancing as may be credible.

The crucial dance images in *Pictures from Brueghel* not only evoke Brueghel's great recreation of the vitality of peasant life which distinguishes his paintings but recall Williams's own earlier tribute to the painter, "The Dance." The poem itself is a single image of the dynamized energy he admired in Brueghel:

> In Brueghel's great picture, The Kermess,
> the dancers go round, they go round and
> around, the squeal and the blare and the
> tweedle of bagpipes, a bugle and fiddles
> tipping their bellies (round as the thick-
> sided glasses whose wash they impound)
> their hips and their bellies off balance
> to turn them. Kicking and rolling about
> the Fair grounds, swinging their butts, those
> shanks must be sound to bear up under such

rollicking measures, prance as they dance
in Brueghel's great picture, The Kermess.

We are struck first by the sheer lustiness, vitality, and sexuality of the dancers: kicking, rolling, swinging their butts, they are hardly graceful or beautiful. Yet their very artlessness is the reality Brueghel chooses for his subject and his "great picture" preserves in art not merely the music and the "rollicking measures" but their *life*. Thus through Brueghel's great imagination and Williams's own, all art (painting, music, poetry) comes to share this third world. Williams's poem is an interesting dance composition itself. The first line is repeated at the end to reinforce the initiation and ending of the dance: we dance *round* to the beginning even as the dancers themselves "go round and/around." None of the lines is end-stopped and we move uninterruptedly through the "round dance" with the musicians and the dancers. The internal rhymes, the alliteration, and the strong verbs serve to create a pattern, despite the off balances of the hips and bellies. In fact, the poem subtly testifies to the dancers' ability to transcend their own awkwardness. They "prance as they dance"—an image of capering gaiety superior to the crude sensuality of their gestures. "The Dance," a joyous celebration by simple people of their own power and healthy gregariousness, would become for Williams the great, tragic deficiency of modern life. How understandable, then, his bitterness at the Puritan fathers for perverting that natural dance at Merry Mount! The volume of poems, *Pictures from Brueghel*, published in 1949, would affirm again and again, in images of dancing people, the need to recover the spirit of those early peasants in "Brueghel's great picture, The Kermess."

From the very beginning of the volume, the images of motion that convey Brueghel's sense of felt life "crowded on canvas" become equated with birth, death, and rebirth into art. So it is that Icarus's fall coincides with the farmer ploughing his field: "the whole pageantry/of the year was/

awake tingling/near"; and though Icarus's splash was "quite unnoticed" Brueghel captured the moment in his painting. In "The Wedding Dance in the Open Air," it is the artist who disciplines the dancers to "go round and round." The Kermess dancers are recreated in the gay rabble, the "ample-bottomed doxies"; and the dance in the market square is gay, lusty, innocent, crudely artless but celebrating the rite of marriage.

> they prance or go openly
> toward the wood's
> edges
>
> round and around in
> rough shoes and
> farm breeches
>
> mouths agape
> Oya!
> kicking up their heels

Williams has chosen the triadic measure to discipline his own recreation of the "riotously gay" scene. Throughout these poems, the painter-artist-poet arranges the scene, much as Williams would in "The Desert Music" once the paralysis of the imagination had passed. Thus in another poem Brueghel patterns the skaters, includes "no detail extraneous/to the composition" and makes art of the spontaneous, earthy gestures of the real world.

In "Children's Games" Brueghel's genius conveys his theme that "everything is motion," and the children are, indeed, the dancers: "Little girls/whirling their skirts about/until they stand out flat/tops pinwheels/to run in the wind with," or their "feet together kicking/through which a boy must pass," and it is their "imagination equilibrium"—the "desperate toys/of children" which makes their dance possible. In "3 Stances" Elaine, Erica, and Emily assume dance poses in a poem whose triadic measure complements their gestures. The first poem anticipates Elaine's dance as she poises for the leap into freedom. Barefoot and graceful, she is caught in the breathless moment before she flees: "calves beginning to flex/wrists/set for the getaway." Erica evokes rich and enigmatic expectation: "the rest remains a/mystery/ your snub nose spinning/on the bridge of it/points the way/ inward." Emily's long legs of a dancer, "built/to carry high/ the small head," create an image of grace and beauty, "gives/ the dance as/your genius" and offers the poet the occasion to capture the "Beautiful Thing" in the moment of stasis. The dance's *promise* is breathlessly prefigured in the delicacy and beauty of the awakening experience: each poem ends, as it were, at the poised leap.

Williams's second poem called "The Dance" transforms that promise into a rich point/counterpoint of cosmic and human experience that is fused through a network of dance images. The poem opens with a familiar image of dancing snowflakes, the "two and two to make a dance"—a harmony out of the chaos of falling snow. Instantly, the poet imagines other forms of the dance: the mind that "dances with itself," the lovers who move two by two in rhythmic harmony unless "you break away and run/the dance is over." Though partners may change and another lover "whirls and glides until he too/leaves off" another always takes his place and "only the dance is sure!" At the close of the poem, the poet affirms the inexorable necessity of the dance that seizes us whether in the recesses of our natures or in the "spinning face to face" with others:

> But only the dance is sure!
> make it your own.
> Who can tell
> what is to come of it?
>
> in the woods of your
> own nature whatever

twig interposes, and bare twigs
have an actuality of their own

this flurry of the storm
that holds us, plays with us and discards us
dancing, dancing as may be credible.

Early in his life, in a moment of despair, Williams had written: "Lean on my shoulder, little one . . . I will lead you to
fields you know nothing of. There's small dancing left for us
any way you look at it." But on another day recorded by
Kora in Hell, he insists that "one must dance nevertheless as
he can." Here, in *Pictures from Brueghel*, confirming his own
belief that the dance will lift us toward flight like the young
girls in "Perpetuum Mobile" into another realm of art: the
picture and the poem, he urges:

Satyrs dance!
    all the deformities take wing
. . . .
Dreams possess me
    and the dance
      of my thoughts

Ultimately, in *Pictures from Brueghel*, the dance will become
the activity of the imagination—as all deformities take wing
to reveal the radiant gist, the Beautiful Thing, the poem of
Williams's third world.

The dance in Williams's long poems "Asphodel, That
Greeny Flower" and "The Desert Music" is the energizing
activity of the imagination as it seeks to transform the world
of things into "objects of wonder" through the creation of the
poem. Both poems are a culmination of Williams's lifelong
aesthetic goal to integrate into the third world of art the
disparities of his experience: the ugliness, pain, debasement,
and dullness of routine life and the elusive, ineffable, creative

surge of that other reality—the objects of the mind. The problem set forth in *Paterson* serves to characterize the search for wholeness and harmony in both poems:

> "Rigor of beauty is the quest. But how
> will you find beauty when it is locked
> in the mind past all remonstrance?"

The route Dr. Paterson follows through the tawdry world of Paterson, the past and the present, the mind and the facts, in search of the "Beautiful Thing" *hidden* in all reality is traced microcosmically in both shorter poems.

Interesting parallels reveal themselves instantly as the two poems commence with the urgent call to the artist, document with the specificity we'll find in *Paterson* the polarities of Williams's experience, and introduce the ritual movement from death to rebirth as the poet seeks, through the dance of the mind, to advance from stasis to creativity. Stimulated by the conviction, as he wrote in "Shadows" that

> The instant
> trivial as it is
> is all we have
> unless—unless
> things the imagination feeds upon,
> the scent of the rose,
> startle us anew.

> —the dance begins: to end about a form
> propped motionless—on the bridge between
> Juarez and El Paso

Thus "The Desert Music" posits the conflicting conditions of the artistic quest: the *dance* and the *motionless form* and, borrowing Crane's fusing image, the bridge that dancing will effect. "How shall we get said what must be said?/Only the

166

poem," Williams declares; and the urgent necessity to write the poem ("I wanted to write a poem/That you would understand.") becomes a major theme at the outset of the journey:

> Only the counted poem, to an exact measure:
> to imitate, not to copy nature, not
> to copy nature
>
> not, prostrate, to copy nature
>   but a dance! to dance
> two and two with him—
>   sequestered there asleep,
>   right end up!
>
>   A music
> supersedes his composure, hallooing to us
> across the great distance . .
>
>   wakens the dance
> who blows upon his benumbed fingers!

The motionless form—that pitiful, debased shard of humanity—to be brought back to life by the dancing poet will become the "matter" of the poem. But though the poet knows that "following insensate music,/is based on the dance:/an agony of self-realization/ bound into a whole/by what which surrounds us," he becomes impotent himself, unable yet "to tell/what subsequently I saw and what heard" until released by the vulgar dancing of the stripper in the Mexican bar. After the misery, the exploitation, the crassness, the obscenity of poverty, dirt, and disease, the stripper's dance is a stirring of the "giants in the dirt."

> One is moved but not
> at the dull show.
> . . . .
> The music!
> I like her. She fits
> the music.

He asks himself in wonder:

> What in the form of an old whore in
> a cheap Mexican joint in Juarez, her bare
> can waggling crazily can be
> so refreshing to me, raise to my ear
> so sweet a tune, built of such slime?

The "desert music" within him awakens as he approaches the bridge near the close of the journey and he hears

> the music! the
> *music*! as when Casals struck
> and held a deep cello tone
> and I am speechless

On the bridge, seeing the lifeless form again in all its tortured ugliness, he knows he must include it in his own beginning music and his dance.

> There it sat
> in the projecting angle of the bridge flange
> as I stood aghast and looked at it—
> in the half-light: shapeless or rather returned
> to its original shape, armless, legless,
> headless, packed like the pit of a fruit into
> that obscure corner—or
> a fish to swim against the stream—or
> a child in the womb prepared to imitate life,
> warding its life against
> a birth of awful promise.

The images of birth that illuminate the motionless mass huddled on the bridge prefigure the poet's emergent self as he identifies his song, his dance, himself!

> I *am* a poet! I
> am. I am. I am a poet, I reaffirmed, ashamed
>
> Now the music volleys through as in
> a lonely moment I hear it. Now it is all
> about me. The dance! The verb detaches itself
> seeking to become articulate
>
> And I could not help thinking
> of the wonders of the brain that
> hears that music and of our
> skill sometimes to record it.

The form of the poem complements his poetic quest: we begin and end on the bridge, as he announces in the early lines. The triadic measure with its variations suggest both the chaos of the raw experience as it unfolds in Mexico and the "measure" or pattern affirmed by the poem. The fragments of conversation float with the fragments of peasant life: the "dried peppers, onions, print goods" and a sense of *wandering* aimlessly is conveyed in the broken lines. The desert music *is* indeed a broken melody until the dance of the stripper calls up "another music," until the poet-doctor finally penetrates that "mucus" to bring about the "birth" at the close of the poem and celebrates that thrust of new life. Both the music and the dance of "The Desert Music" are touched with that aura of inviolable beauty, that rare moment of apotheosis in Williams's poetry, when he is humbled by his own "skill sometimes" to raise the "Beautiful Thing" from its secret hiding place, to record it in that eternal dance he confirms in art.

"Asphodel, That Greeny Flower" is, on one level, a tribute to Flossie and the restorative power of love viewed over a lifetime of shared experience. On another, it is a celebration of the creative power of the imagination, that, "approaching death," he can still affirm:

> . . . love and the imagination
> are of a piece,
>   swift as the light
> to avoid destruction.

The presence of Williams's three worlds, the things—imaged in the wooden, odorless asphodel; the idea—that dance of the mind remembering, endowing with beauty, recreating; and the poem—the song: "I come, my sweet,/to sing to you," conjoin in a trinity that echoes in the form of the poem: three books, three lines of Williams's triadic measure, three central images: the flower, the sea, the dance. The themes of "Asphodel" had preoccupied him most of his life: the wondrous "discovery" of "flowers in Hell"; the veneration of the imagination and the compulsion to write the poem; the ritual cycles in nature and men's lives of death and rebirth illuminated by the power of art to defy that cycle: "I bring you,/reawakened,/a memory of flowers," so that the poet reminds us:

> It is difficult
> to get the news from poems
>   yet men die miserably every day
>   for lack
> of what is found there.

The world's loss of the dance and the need to recapture it is related to the loss of love and the urge to recover it through the aid of the imaginative faculties. "We danced,/in our minds,/and read a book together,/You remember?" he reminds Flossie. Elsewhere, the dance is the shimmering motion of the sea: "The poem/if it reflects the sea/reflects only/its dance/upon that profound depth/where/it seems to triumph," a dance lost with the explosion of the bomb "dedicated to our destruction." Juxtaposing the death force of the modern world to the creative force that discovered America, Williams plays again on the motif of the ruined garden; "how bitter/a disappointment!" in the abortion of such promise:

170

> For there had been kindled
> more minds
> than that of the discoverers
> and set dancing
> to a measure,
> a new measure!
> Soon lost.
> The measure itself
> has been lost
> and we suffer for it.

What he carries to her is the sense of the reawakening earth
that stirred him to proclaim in his youth: "The whole world/
became my garden." In the Coda to "Asphodel" Williams
brings together the harsh realities of the world: death, the
bomb, the thunderstroke, the darkness, the controversy, and
the odorless flower with the light, memory, youth, possibility, the imagination, and the "girl so pale/and ready to faint"
at the wedding:

> Inseparable from the fire
> its light
> Takes precedence over it.

Even the colt "kicks up its heels" in that magic, ephemeral
moment of awareness when "only the imagination is real!" So
he enjoins the companion of his age, "let us love/confident as
is the light/in its struggle with darkness." At the close of
"Asphodel" poet-husband-lover affirms the transformation of
ordinary things to the truly precious objects our minds shape
them into:

> Asphodel
> has no odor
> save to the imagination
> but it too
> celebrates the light.

The final image is one of movement, as the perfume of the asphodel revives for him and begins to "penetrate/into all crevices/of my world." Thus the commitment to love becomes the commitment to art—indeed his *act of love* for Flossie, the world, and himself. Though "Asphodel" is more of a song than a dance, the verbs that move the poem on its way speak for Williams's constant faith in the efficacy of motion, even now to an old man "whose bones/have the movement/of the sea," who could declare finally: "It is all/a celebration of the light."

It would be unwise, perhaps, to impose a pattern of imagery on *Paterson*, given Dr. Williams's own injunction. Yet some patterns emerge from the seemingly unsynthesized five books that suggest a unity beyond Williams's own loose arrangement of "ideas and things." The distinct mythic qualities of the poem were set forth in the "Author's Note" in which Williams announced his plan: *"Paterson* is a long poem in four parts—that a man is himself a city, beginning, seeking, achieving and concluding his life in ways which the various aspects of the city may embody—if imaginatively conceived—any city." A place and a man, Paterson comes to symbolize other voyagers who seek his goal in the modern world: "Rigor of beauty is the quest." The great sweep of the poem offers us several perspectives: the mythic, the historical, the contemporary Paterson—urban sprawl and industrial wasteland. But Paterson is also the whole modern world, and the Beautiful Thing has, as we discover in Book Three, "an identity/surmounting the world." The images associated with each of these perspectives do, in fact, form a mosaic and relate the several fragments to each other—the "prose" and "poetry" of it. One such image is the Passaic River; another, Sam Patch's leap into the falls; another, the "radiant gist"; another, Paterson's journey—as he walks or drives—moving from primordial time of beginnings with the sleeping giants to historical time, both past and present. Energizing all of these perspectives are images of dynamic motion, at times expressed in the crashing falls, at times conveyed through the ritual movements of a dance. Thus the dance is a motif in *Paterson*, one of several equations for potentiality, for meaningful activity. Since the dark vision of the first four books prevails, it is not surprising that actual dances belong to past experience or are veiled from the unperceiving inhabitants of the city. Dr. Paterson himself experiences in the present only a tragic void, the divorce that is everywhere in contemporary America. The tragic reality is the divorce of the people from the land, from their history, from each other. Lacking a language for communication, an inability to confront life and death, and sickened by a paralyzed will, by perversion, and by "the eternal stony, ungrateful and unpromising dirt they lived by" they can ask only, mildly perplexed, "Geez, Doc . . . what the hell does it mean?"

Yet the key to renewal is always present: in the words and the courage to use them; in "pulling the disparates together to clarify/and compress"; in knowing that "without invention nothing is well spaced"; in understanding that "memory is a kind of accomplishment/a sort of renewal"; and in accepting the descent "made up of despairs/and without accomplishment" that "realizes a new awakening." Finally, in the rediscovery of the "GIST"/INvenshun" lies the recognition that "the world/of the imagination most endures." But these are only hints and guesses to the people of Paterson who know only the "virgins and the whores," sensing nothing of "art alone, male and female, a field of/flowers, a tapestry, spring flowers unequaled/in loveliness." Dr. Paterson's own faith in the "eternal return" in nature, experience, and art ebbs and flows but finally leads him out of the chaos of Paterson to transform the "giant in the dirt." As Guimond observes, "To be fully alive and creative . . . men must be open and receptive to everything around them. They cannot ignore any of the material forces inside or outside themselves, no matter how alien or destructive . . . disorder also feeds art."[19]

At the end of *Paterson*, he affirms his beginnings and the journey that has not been in vain:

The (self) direction has been changed
    the serpent
          its tail in its mouth
"the river has returned to its beginnings"
    and backward
          (and forward)
it tortures itself within me
      until time has been washed finally under:
         and "I knew all (or enough)
it became me   "

The "Preface" to *Paterson* evokes the resurrection myth
that frames Dr. Paterson's entire journey both through the
contemporary world and through the world of his unconscious as he seeks to be born. The mythic quest is anticipated
in the question posed by the anonymous guide: a kind of
Virgil to Paterson's Dante. "But how will you find beauty
when it is locked in the mind past all remonstrance?" The
answer lies in the efforts to "unlock," release, bring to birth:
"rolling up out of chaos,/a nine months' wonder, the city/the
man, an identity—" As Williams well knew, the activity attending parturition is violent, irreversible, "an interpenetra-
tion, both ways." The verbs image an almost relentless motion as the poem seeks to be born, as the "events dancing
two/and two with language" strive toward a new order, a
new life, even though dawns are "tangled in darkness."

To make a start
out of particulars
and make them general, rolling
up the sum, by defective means
. . . .
For the beginning is assuredly
the end—since we know nothing, pure
and simple, beyond
our own complexities:

174

The man, the poet "renews himself/thereby, in addition and subtraction,/walking up and down." At the end of the Preface, introducing the images of fragment and flow that will mark Paterson's voyage through the city, the omniscient guide observes the cyclic path of the particles of moisture which return upon themselves like the river itself:

> divided as the dew,
> floating mists, to be rained down and
> regathered into a river that flows
> and encircles:

These images of dynamic movement occur with frequency throughout *Paterson* and always hint of a direction, an intimation of the descent that "beckons/as the ascent beckoned." The swirling waters of the Passaic and the rushing falls are poetic counterparts of Paterson's thoughts—creative, life-giving:

> Jostled as are the waters approaching
> the brink, his thoughts
> interlace, repel and cut under,
> rise rock-thwarted and turn aside
> but forever strain forward—

And Sam Patch's leap into the falls is his own leap into the filthy Passaic:

> He became a national hero in '28, '29 and
> toured the country diving from cliffs and
> masts, rocks and bridges—to prove his thesis:
> Some things can be done as well as others.

When Patch finally plunges to his death, it is described as a kind of graceful ballet: "instead of descending with a plummet-like fall his body wavered in the air—"

a sort of springtime
toward which their minds aspired
but which he saw,
within himself—ice bound

and leaped, "the body, not until
the following spring, frozen in
an ice cake"

Thus Sam Patch's "resurrection" comes in the spring of the year when they found him frozen in the ice-cake.

But in the prosaic "present" of Paterson, the elemental antithesis serves only to emphasize the "divorce" at the core of human experience. The miracle of the waters rippling in response to the moving air, "touching as the mind touches" but "never mingling," stands in sharp contrast to the "separate worlds" of things and ideas which spin forward, destined forever to be divided.

And the air lying over the water
lifts the ripples, brother
to brother, touching as the mind touches,
counter-current, upstream
brings in the fields, hot and cold
parallel but never mingling, one that whirls
backward at the brink and curls invisibly
upward, fills the hollow, whirling,
an accompaniment—but apart, observant of
the distress, sweeps down or up clearing
the spray—
            brings in the rumors of separate
worlds. . . .

The harmonious "whirling" and "curling upward" testify to the coexistence of opposites in nature, "brother to brother"— a condition alien to the world of Paterson with its "divisions and imbalances." As Dr. Paterson, in his perambulations, witnesses that "divorce" between nature and man, he is blocked by the dullness that "overlays the world." As he "drives/his new car out to the suburbs" or walks through the city streets "foot pacing foot outward/into emptiness," he *is*, as he wrote early in *Kora* "Persephone gone to hell." But still a man must "WALK in the world" to find "that secret world,/a sphere, a snake with its tail in its mouth" which rolls "backward into the past."

The significant dancing, then, in *Paterson* occurs in several historical prose fragments. The primitive Indian death rite, the dance of the Kinte Kaye, Williams recounts, was a religious use among the savages. Thus the brave danced "the Kinte Kaye all the time," while they "mutilated him, and at last cut off his head." The death dance had transforming powers, for after the dead chieftain was laid upon the sacred burial spot, the funeral procession performed the Kinte Kaye in sadness. No such ritual attends the old hag's dance on Sunday in the park. Yet, as Williams asked in *Kora*,

They are the same men they always were—but fallen.
Do they dance now, they that danced beside Helicon?
They dance much as they did then, only, few have an
eye for it—through the dirt and fumes.

Paterson watches the dancing and takes away something of its mystery:

—lifts one arm holding the cymbals
of her thoughts, cocks her old head
and dances! raising her skirts:

La la la la !
. . . .
This is the old, the very old, upon old,
the undying: even to the minute gestures,

the hand holding the cup, the wine
spilling, the arm stained by it:
. . . .

—the leg raised, verisimilitude
even to the coarse contours of the leg, the
bovine touch! The leer, the cave of it,
the female of it facing the male, the satyr—
    (Priapus!)
with the lonely implication, goatherd
and goat, fertility, the attack, drunk,
cleansed

The dance of the "undying" in the park touches upon a
familiar motif in Williams's dance—the cleansing rites of the
mythic satyr. Here for a moment are the lusty modern ver-
sions of those age-old celebrants dancing in honor of Priapus,
god of sexual passion, son of Aphrodite and Zeus and known
to some as Eros. And the drunken orgy in the park stimu-
lates his own momentary perception: "We leap awake and
what we see/fells us." We recall those words in *Kora*: "They
dance much as they did then, only few have an eye for it,
through the dirt and fumes." *His* awareness impels him further in his search:

> But somehow a man must lift himself
> again—
>   again is the magic word
>   turning the in out
> Speed against the inundation
>   is a fine balance

A tension exists between the tragic reality and the infinite
potential: between the debased naked dancing in the speak-
easy, the dance of the lesbians, the vulgar dance with the
prostitutes, on the one hand, and the primitive beauty of the
Kinte Kaye, Bessie Smith, and black dancing on the other.

178

Williams's prose fragment, Mezz Mezzrow's account of the Blues, raises an interesting parallel with his own conception of art. We might remember that the "Blues" arose out of the tension between circumstance and possibility. Robert Bone noted:

> The grim reality that gives them birth bespeak the limits and restrictions, the barriers and thwartings, which the universe opposed to human will. But the tough response that is the blues bespeaks a moral courage, a spiritual freedom, a sense of human possibility, which more than balances the scales.[20]

Structurally, the form and the freedom of blues and jazz reflect the duality posed by despair and exultation, enslavement and release.

Williams's fragment touches on the possibility as well as the despair in Bessie Smith's "moanful stories and the patterns of true harmony." Such dancing as the black man danced, his joy and his despair, is to touch some truth in a dislocated world. And the dance and Bessie's songs are art:

> . . . and white man . . . could sing and dance and play with the Negro. You didn't have to take the finest and most original and honest music in America and mess it up because you were a white man; you could dig the colored man's real message and get in there with him . . . Man, I was gone with it—inspiration's mammy was with me. . . . I was put in a trance by Bessie's moanful stories and the patterns of true harmony in the piano background, full of little runs that crawled up and down my spine like mice. Every note that woman wailed vibrated on the tight strings of my nervous system: every word she sang answered a question I was asking.

We have no way of knowing whether Williams was familiar with the basic pattern of the blues, a rhythm and harmony composed of three common chords: the tonic triad, the subdominant triad, and the dominant seventh. The recurrent pattern of three, close in spirit to Williams's variable foot, appeared most generally to be the repetition of the first line in the second, followed by an improvisation and variation of rhythm in the third. Thus blues and jazz both depended on a delicate balance between form and variation—a pattern Williams believed to be the essence of his new "line."

Following the prose account of Rapp, the Rhythm Kings, and Bessie Smith, the familiar Williams satyrs reappear:

> . . . or the Satyrs, a
> pre-tragic play,
> a satyric play!
> All plays
> were satyric when they were most devout.
> Ribald as a satyr!
>
> Satyrs dance!
> all the deformities take wing

And in Paterson's mind, the dance finally becomes the dynamism of the imagination as it weds dream to reality and makes the poetry that brings all dances together:

> Dream possess me
> and the dance
> of my thoughts

As Hillis Miller remarks on this passage: "Time has been transcended and all the elements of the poem are there together, touching one another, interacting with one another. . . . The symbol for this unification is the dance. The elements of the poet's world circle around one another in harmonious measure."[21] *Paterson* ends with the perfect blending in the *poem* of music, dance, words; all art *and* the life which art "imitates" ("to imitate, not to copy nature"):

The measure intervenes, to measure is all we know,
    a choice among measures . .
        the measured dance
"unless the scent of a rose
        startle us anew"
. . . .
We know nothing and can know nothing
                     but
the dance, to dance to a measure
contrapuntally,
        Satyrically, the tragic foot.

Except for the desperate gyrations of the prostitutes, "high heels, click, click," who have no sense of their own innocence in the stench of the city, dancing in Williams's *Paterson* conjures up the multiple associations inherent in his dance from earlier notions of "Persephone gone to hell." Dance is the efficacious activity of the gods, the deities of fertility and plenitude: Dionysus, Pan, Priapus, the satyrs who dance our tragic deformities into the graceful, the "Beautiful Thing." Dance is intrinsic to the motions of the river, the falls, the flow of time turning back ends to beginnings. Dance is the rite and play of primitive man who had the sense of integration lost to the modern, fragmented world. And finally, dance is the *measure*, the rhythmic pattern of all art that encloses the past and present into a permanent, enduring reality:

        —the virgin and the whore, which
        most endures? the world
        of the imagination most endures:

        Pollack's blobs of paint sqeezed out
        with design! Nothing else
        is real . . .

And real, too, the ubiquitous Dr. Paterson: satyr-poet-dancer whose imagination, as he wrote in "To Elsie," "strains/after deer/going by fields of goldenrod in/the stifling heat of September." But we are not destroyed, as Williams prophesied then, for the same imagination captures the "isolate flecks" in which "something is given off," and we follow the poet who flings himself "into the other dance, to the other music." We follow Williams Carlos Williams into his third world:

> from all that division and
> subtraction a measure
> toe and heel
>
> heel and toe he felt
> as if he had
> been dancing

NOTES

1. Whittemore, *William Carlos Williams*, 1975, p. 52.

2. Powell Woods, "William Carlos Williams: The Poet as Engineer," in *Profile of William Carlos Williams*, ed. Mazzaro, 1971, p. 85.

3. Ernst Cassirer, *The Philosophy of Symbolic Forms*, vol. II: *Mythical Thought*, tr. Ralph Manheim (New York: Yale University Press, 1955), p. 74.

4. These and other observations following in Miller, *Poets of Reality*, 1969, p. 291 ff.

5. Rexroth, *American Poetry in the Twentieth Century*, 1973, p. 77.

6. Miller, p. 191 ff.

7. Whittemore, p. 199.

8. Ibid., p. 285.

9. Miller, p. 327.

10. Guimond, *The Art of William Carlos Williams*, 1968, p. 60.

11. Cassirer, p. 40.

12. Philip Gerber, "So Much Depends: The Williams Foreground," in Mazzaro, pp. 9 ff.

13. Mircea Eliade, *Cosmos and History: The Myth of the Eternal Return* (New York: Harper, 1949), p. 23.

14. Miller, p. 314.

15. Williams, *Selected Letters*, ed. Thirwall, 1957, p. 8.

16. Townley, *The Early Poetry of William Carlos Williams*, 1972, p. 89.

17. Burke, *The Philosophy of Literary Form*, 1941, pp. 8–12.

18. Guimond, p. 230.

19. Ibid., p. 25.

20. Robert Bone, "Ralph Ellison and the Uses of Imagination," in *Anger and Beyond*, ed. Herbert Hill, 1966, p. 91.

21. Miller, p. 256.

Afterword

This study began with the discovery that dance images recur in the poetry of four first-rank American poets. The question to be asked finally is whether the choice of such an image for modern poetry has been felicitous. Certainly, the association of dancer and poet is an old alliance; here in a Hindu poem that dates back to 1500 B.C. the poet celebrates the sacred dance:

> His form is everywhere: all pervading in His Siva-Sakti:
> Chidambaram is everywhere, everywhere His dance:
> As Siva is all and omnipresent.
> Everywhere is Siva's gracious dance made manifest.
> His five-fold dances are temporal and timeless.
> . . . .
> Our Lord dances His eternal dance.

Each of the poets whose work I have examined acknowledged generously his debt to the past; each was aware of the potentiality of the dance to define both man's orientation in the physical world and his attempt to transform that world through art. In a modern society that no longer created myth and that discarded faith, in which rituals were no longer efficacious, the need to recreate "something of value" through art encouraged the poet to rekindle an age-old reverence for the dance.

Each of the poets was experimental by instinct. While at times the effort to invoke the dance was awkward and unconvincing, more often the achieved effects comprised a perfect integration of theme and form. When Eliot's awareness of "the dance along the artery" reflected in the "drift of stars" is echoed in the lyrical beauty of these lines in "Burnt Norton," we share the intensity of the moment, the vision itself. Elsewhere, when Eliot presses the dance image in the early Saint Narcissus poem, neither the frenzy of the dancer nor the preachy quality of the message—"He could not live men's ways"—enhances the dance itself: "So he became a dancer to God." Only when Eliot juxtaposes dramatically the notion of "possibility" with the crushing *knowledge* of reality, in the contrapuntal rhythms examined earlier, is his double vision of the dance particularly effective. Eliot's correlative for the dance emanates from a Dantean "Higher Dream" more often than not thwarted. Dance as a ritual of transcendence "never here to be realized" adds a poignancy to his poetry that we have come to associate with his tragic vision. He is not the poet of *Paradiso*, as some of his ardent admirers would have us believe. Indeed, Eliot himself disclaimed the achievement of so lofty a goal as "an occupation for the saint—" More consistently he is the architect of a purgatorial vision: "This way the pilgrimage/Of expiation/Round and round the circle."

In the case of Crane, Roethke, or Williams the success of the dance image grows from the poet's ability to conceive dance on several levels simultaneously: each poet is at once dancing satyr and spiritual shaman. They all relished the erotic aspects of the dance from its inception as well as the hieratic role dance has always played in ritual. They enjoyed the mysterious effects of dancing on the individual:

> . . . I in my north room
> dance naked, grotesquely
> before my mirror
> waving my shirt round my head
> and singing softly to myself:

and their lyrical talents allowed them to wed dance images to verse lines that literally dance across the pages.

In Crane's "Chaplinesque" we *see* Charlie's falls and pirou-
ettes and in "For the Marriage of Faustus and Helen" Crane
successfully recreates the frenetic activity of the Dionysian
revels. Elsewhere, Maquokeeta's cry to "dance us back the
tribal morn!" suffers from Crane's own doubt in this otherwise lyrical and moving vision. In "National Winter Garden"
the pathos that should attend the debased dance of the burlesque queen (a figure close in spirit to Williams's Elsie) is
attenuated by Crane's inappropriate choice of language:
"Then you, the burlesque of our lust—and faith,/Lug us back
lifeward—bone by infant bone." Critics who point to the
breakdown of the middle sections of *The Bridge* also marvel
at Crane's insensitivity to these flaws. Where image and vision are assimilated in the poetry of Hart Crane, the effects
are more successful.

Roethke and Williams, as we have seen, bring dance images to a level of perfection more frequently than Eliot or
Crane. What Eliot would have called their "unified sensibility"—their talent for uniting thought and feeling indissolubly in the dance image—might account for their predilection
to frame experience in the image of the dance. They were
eager to explore, further than their predecessors, nonverbal
equivalents for their deepest, most inexpressible states. Aes-
thetically, they would have agreed with Pound's observation,
"Music rots when it gets too far from the dance. Poetry
atrophies when it gets too far from music." But their poetry
is more visual than aural: we are made to *see* the dancers that
people *Paterson* in the same way that we envisage the young
boy whirled round and round on his father's toes in "My
Papa's Waltz." Both Roethke and Williams talked and wrote
about the uses of the dance for poetry, and both created a
poetry that dancers themselves could appropriate as their
own.

The four poets I have explored in this book were remarkable in their willingness to give words to gesture, in their
confidence that the ephemeral experience of the dance could

be made permanent without losing its vital dynamism, and in their enthusiasm and respect for the art of the dance.

One final note . . . the dance image is successful only when the harmonizing imagination of the poet brings all other poetic components to bear upon his experience. An image, however brilliant, is part of a poetic whole encompassing scaffold, language, and rhythm. When the poets whose work I have examined held in perfect tension all elements at their disposal, when they understood the indivisible nature of those elements, they made memorable contributions to American poetry. It is this integrity Yeats understood, in the lines which would appear to be a fitting coda to this book:

> O chestnut-tree, great-rooted blossomer,
> Are you the leaf, the blossom or the bole?
> O body swayed to music, O brightening glance,
> How can we know the dancer from the dance?

Primary Sources

Hart Crane
The Letters of Hart Crane, 1916–32. Ed. Brom Weber. New York: Liveright, 1952.
The Complete Poems and Selected Letters and Prose of Hart Crane. Ed. Brom Weber. New York: Liveright, 1966.

T. S. Eliot
The Sacred Wood. London: Methuen, 1920.
Selected Essays. New York: Harcourt, Brace & Co. 1932.
"The Ballet," *Criterion* 5, no. 3 (1922–39).
The Complete Poems and Plays, 1909–1950. New York: Harcourt Brace and World, 1952.
On Poetry and Poets. New York: Farrar, Straus, and Cudahy, 1957.
To Criticize the Critic. New York: Farrar, Straus, and Giroux, 1965.
The Waste Land, A Facsimile and Transcript of the Original Drafts Including the Annotations of Ezra Pound. Ed. Valerie Eliot. New York: Harcourt, Brace, Javanovich, 1971.

Theodore Roethke
The Collected Poems of Theodore Roethke. New York: Doubleday, 1966.
Selected Letters of Theodore Roethke. Ed. Ralph Mills. Seattle: University of Washington Press, 1968.
Straws from the Fire: From the Notebooks of Theodore Roethke. Ed. David Wagoner. New York: Doubleday, 1972.

William Carlos Williams
The Autobiography of William Carlos Williams. New York: New Directions, 1948.

Primary Sources

The Collected Later Poems of William Carlos Williams. New York: New Directions, 1950.

Selected Essays of William Carlos Williams. New York: Random House, 1951.

In the American Grain. New York: New Directions, 1956.

The Selected Letters of William Carlos Williams. Ed. John C. Thirwall. New York: McDowell, Obolensky, 1957.

I Wanted to Write A Poem. Ed. Edith Heal. Boston: Beacon, 1958.

Paterson. New York: New Directions, 1958.

Pictures from Brueghel and Other Poems. New York: New Directions, 1962.

The Collected Earlier Poetry of William Carlos Williams. New York: New Directions, 1966.

Imaginations. New York: New Directions, 1970.

Selected Bibliography

Allen, Gay Wilson, and Davis, Charles T. *Walt Whitman's Poems.* New York: New York University Press, 1955.

Balakian, Anna. *The Symbolist Movement.* New York: Random House, 1967.

Blessing, Richard Allen. *Theodore Roethke's Dynamic Vision.* Bloomington: Indiana University Press, 1974.

Burke, Kenneth. *The Philosophy of Literary Form.* New York: Random House, 1941.

Campbell, Joseph. *The Hero with a Thousand Faces.* Cleveland: World, 1956.

Cassirer, Ernst. *An Essay on Man.* New York: Doubleday Anchor, 1944.

———. *Language and Myth.* Translated by Susanne K. Langer. New York: Dover, 1946, p. 22.

———. *The Philosophy of Symbolic Forms,* vols. I and II. New Haven: Yale University Press, 1953.

Chase, Richard. *Quest for Myth.* Baton Rouge: Louisiana State University Press, 1949.

Davies, Sir John. "Orchestra." In *Poetry of the English Renaissance, 1509–1660.* New York: F. S. Crofts, 1945.

Dembo, L. S. *Conceptions of Reality in Modern Poetry.* Berkeley: University of California Press, 1942.

Dickey, James. Review of *Sequence, Sometimes Metaphysical, Poetry,* November 1964.

Drew, Elizabeth. *T. S. Eliot: The Design of His Poetry.* New York: Scribner's, 1949.

Duncan, Isadora. *My Life.* New York: Horace Liveright, 1927.

Eastman, Max. "Isadora Duncan Is Dead," *Nation* 125, 3247 (September 1927).

Eliade, Mircea. *Myth and Reality.* Translated by William R. Trask. New York: Harper & Row, 1963.

Ellis, Havelock. *The Dance of Life*. Boston: Houghton Mifflin, 1923.

Flaubert, Gustave. *Madame Bovary*. Translated by Francis Steegmuller. New York: Modern Library, 1957.

Frank, Joseph. "Spatial Form in Modern Literature." In *Criticism, The Foundations of Modern Literary Judgment*. Edited by Mark Schorer, Josephine Miles, and Gordon McKenzie. New York: Harcourt, Brace, 1948.

Frye, Northrop. *Anatomy of Criticism*. New York: Atheneum Press, 1966.

Graham, Martha. *The Dance in America*, TV Program, 14 April 1976. New York.

Graves, Robert. *The Greek Myths*, vol. II. Baltimore: Penguin, 1955.

Guimond, James. *The Art of William Carlos Williams*. Urbana: University of Illinois Press, 1968.

Hall, James B., and Ulanov, Barry, eds. *Modern Culture and the Arts*. New York: McGraw-Hill, 1967.

Heilman, Robert. "Theodore Roethke: Personal Notes." *Shenandoah*, Autumn 1964.

Hill, Herbert, ed. *Anger and Beyond: The Negro Writer in the U.S.* New York: Harper & Row, 1966.

Horton, Philip. *Hart Crane: The Life of an American Poet*. New York: W. W. Norton, 1937.

Jones, Genesius. *Approach to the Purpose*. London: Hodder & Stoughton, 1964.

Jung, Carl. *Man and His Symbols*. New York: Laurel, 1964.

Kenner, Hugh. *The Pound Era*. Berkeley: University of California Press, 1971.

Kermode, Frank. *Romantic Image*. New York: Vintage, 1957.

Kirstein, Lincoln. *Dance, A Short History of Classic Theatrical Dancing*. New York: Garden City Publishing Company, 1935.

Kunitz, Stanley. "Poet of Transformations." *The New Republic*, 23 January 1965.

———. "Theodore Roethke." *New York Review of Books*, 17 October 1963.

Langer, Susanne K. *Problems of Art*. New York: Scribner's, 1951.

Leibowitz, Herbert. *Hart Crane*. New York: Columbia University Press, 1968.

Levi, Albert. *Literature, Philosophy, and the Imagination*. Bloomington: Indiana University Press, 1962.

Lewis, R. W. B. *The Poetry of Hart Crane*. Princeton: Princeton University Press, 1968.

Lloyd, Margaret. *The Borzoi Book of Modern Dance*. New York: Knopf, 1949.

Macdougall, Allan Ross. *Isadora: A Revolutionary in Art and Love*. Edinburgh: Thos. Nelson, 1960.

MacNeice, Louis. *The Poetry of William Butler Yeats*. New York: Oxford University Press, 1941.

Maritain, Jacques. *Creative Intuition in Art and Poetry*. New York: World, 1953.

Martin, John. *John Martin's Book of the Dance*. New York: Tudor, 1963.

Matthews, T. S. *Great Tom*. New York: Harper & Row, 1973.

Mazzaro, Jerome, ed. *Profile of William Carlos Williams*. Columbus: Charles E. Merrill, 1971.

Miller, J. Hillis. *Poets of Reality: Six Twentieth-Century Writers*. New York: Atheneum, 1969.

Monroe, Harriet. "Comment." *Poetry* 31, no. 4 (January 1925).

Nietzsche, Friedrich. *The Birth of Tragedy*. Translated by Francis Golffing. New York: Anchor, 1956.

Poems of the Dance. Edited by Edward R. Dickson. New York: Knopf, 1921.

Pound, Ezra. Dedication to Sophokles, *Women of Trachis*. New York: New Directions, 1957.

Pound, Ezra. *Gaudier-Brzeska, A Memoir*. New York: New Directions, 1917.

Quinn, Vincent. *Hart Crane*. New York: Twayne, 1963.

Rexroth, Kenneth. *American Poetry in the Twentieth Century*. New York: Seabury, 1973.

Rosenthal, M. L. *The Modern Poets*. London: Oxford University Press, 1960.

Rubin, Joseph J. *The Historic Whitman*. University Park: Pennsylvania State University Press, 1973.

Sachs, Curt. *World History of the Dance.* Translated by Bessie Schonberg. New York: Seven Arts, 1952.

Sanders, Gerald DeWitt; Nelson, John Herbert; and Rosenthal, M. L., eds. *Chief Modern Poets of Britain and America,* vol. II. London: Macmillan, 1970.

Santayana, George. *Three Philosophical Poets.* New York: Doubleday Anchor, 1938.

Seager, Allan. *The Glass House.* New York: McGraw-Hill, 1968.

Sebeok, Thomas A., ed. *Myth.* Bloomington: Indiana University Press, 1955.

Selden, Elizabeth. *The Dancer's Quest.* Berkeley: University of California Press, 1935.

Schneider, Ilya Ilych. *Isadora Duncan: The Russian Years.* Translated by David Magarshack. New York: Harcourt Brace and World, 1969.

Shawn, Ted. *The American Ballet.* New York: Holt, 1926.

Sorell, Walter, ed. *The Dance Has Many Faces.* Cleveland: World, 1951.

Spears, Monroe K. *Dionysus and the City: Modernism in Twentieth-Century Poetry.* New York: Oxford University Press, 1970.

Symons, Arthur. "The World As Ballet." In *Studies in Seven Arts.* London: Martin Secker, 1924.

Taylor, Margaret Fisk. *A Time to Dance.* Boston: United Church Press, 1967.

Townley, Rod. *The Early Poetry of William Carlos Williams.* Ithaca, N.Y.: Cornell University Press, 1972.

Trachtenberg, Alan. *Brooklyn Bridge, Fact and Symbol.* New York: Oxford University Press, 1965.

Unterecker, John. *Voyager: A Life of Hart Crane.* New York: Farrar, Straus, and Giroux, 1969.

Vickers, Clinton. "Image into Symbol: The Evolution of the Dance in the Poetry and Drama of W. B. Yeats." Unpublished thesis, University of Massachusetts, 1974.

Whittemore, Reed. *William Carlos Williams: Poet from Jersey.* Boston: Houghton Mifflin, 1975.

Mary Wigman in Elizabeth Selden, *The Dancer's Quest.* Berkeley: University of California Press, 1935.

Index

Index